Praise for *GOAL!*

"I strongly recommend *GOAL!* to anyone who wants to increase sales, start their own business, develop a high performance team, or successfully tackle any other important business objective. The key is the book's 30 Day Goal Track, which has you taking action from day one and keeps you on course until your goal is achieved."

—Steve Odland, Chairman & CEO of Office Depot

"Great achievements start with big dreams. Gladys Stone and Fred Whelan have written an extremely practical guide for setting and achieving goals. Those who follow their plan will accomplish much."

—Kim Lopdrup, President of Red Lobster

"*GOAL!* offers a simple, compelling approach to achieving your lifetime business goal:
- Focus—What's that 'One' goal that is life-changing?
- Alignment—Ensuring you are personally committed to the actions you must take.
- Discipline—The 30 Day Road Map to keep you on track."

—Don Knauss, Chairman & CEO of Clorox

"*GOAL!* is an engaging and thoughtful book. It is also very practical. The "phased approach" of the book makes it useful to anyone struggling to formulate and achieve a task. I recommend *GOAL!* to anyone in this circumstance."

—Thomas Gilligan, Dean, McCombs School of Business, University of Texas

"A clear and systematic approach to getting what you want. *GOAL!* not only offers practical, actionable steps for achieving tangible results today, but it will help you establish habits which will pay dividends for years to come. A quick read with meaningful payoff."

—Greg Berglund, President of Mrs. Fields Gifts

"*GOAL!* provides a fresh approach to determining and then accomplishing one's business goals. In order to survive in these uncertain economic times, a systematic approach to goal attainment as outlined in this book becomes increasingly important. *GOAL!* provides good tips that focus on positive approaches, solutions, and mindsets that challenge the reader to implement and follow an action plan that will ultimately enable one to realize his or her goals.

"The book also discusses key elements in being successful in the workplace. For example, *GOAL!* stresses the importance of effective teamwork to maximize performance. It provides a series of exercises for those contemplating a career change, including questions such as 'What do I enjoy doing and what am I good at?' And, in giving direction to individuals whose dream is to start their own business, it discusses the psychological, financial, and creative aspects in launching new business ventures."

> —Conrado (Bobby) M. Gempesaw II, Dean and Professor, Lerner College of Business and Economics, University of Delaware

"The concept of setting goals is one which is practical and most important at a time like this. This book gives the roadmap to follow, done in a timely and realistic manner. Written to help build this roadmap, with great examples, this will be one of those must-reads and must-keeps."

> —James G. Ellis, Dean, Marshall School of Business, University of Southern California

GOAL!

YOUR 30-DAY GAME PLAN FOR BUSINESS AND CAREER SUCCESS

by Gladys Stone and Fred Whelan

Fresno, California

Published by Quill Driver Books
an imprint of Linden Publishing
2006 South Mary
Fresno, California 93721
559-233-6633 / 800-345-4447
QuillDriverBooks.com

Quill Driver Books and Colophon are trademarks of
Linden Publishing, Inc.

To order another copy of this book, please call
1-800-345-4447.

Quill Driver Books Project Cadre:
Doris Hall, John David Marion, Stephen Blake Mettee,
Kent Sorsky, Maura J. Zimmer

ISBN 978-1-884956-95-9 (1-884956-95-5)

135798642

Printed in the United States of America
on acid-free paper.

Library of Congress Cataloging-in-Publication Data

Stone, Gladys.
  Goal! : your 30 day gameplan for business and career success / by Gladys Stone
and Fred Whelan.
     p. cm.
  ISBN-13: 978-1-884956-95-9 (pbk. : alk. paper)
  ISBN-10: 1-884956-95-5 (pbk. : alk. paper)
 1. Goal setting in personnel management. 2. Goal (Psychology) 3. Employee
motivation. 4. Career development--Psychological aspects. I. Whelan, Fred. II.
Title.
  HF5549.5.G6S76 2009
  650.1--dc22
                                        2008055809

Dedicated to
Susan, Morgan and Titi, too

CONTENTS

PHASE I

CHAPTER ONE
Target Your Goal

How would you feel if you knew that accomplishing your business goal was within your grasp? Even an elusive goal that you had tried many times to attain? You would probably be ecstatic at the prospect of finally being able to accomplish it. And you would probably be even more thrilled if you could apply what you learned to reaching your next goal, *knowing* you would be successful.

Whether it's reaching an aggressive sales goal, becoming a better manager, getting a promotion, starting a new business, successfully negotiating for something you want, or being more productive, this book can help you do it. No matter how complex the goal or how elusive it has been in the past, you are only thirty days away from success.

This is what *GOAL!* is all about. It's the little book that helps people in a big way. It offers an effective, straightforward process that will take you from goal identification to goal completion. You will start taking specific action towards your goal within one week's time. At the end of thirty days you will have either accomplished your goal or will be well on your way to doing so. If you are looking to achieve a tangible result to a business goal, this is the book for you.

GOAL! Offers a Systematic Approach to Getting What You Want.

Throughout this book, we will be asking you to write things down. The reason for this is that putting things in writing is an important tool in realizing your goal. Things that are written down are more likely to get done. They become more real and take on a life of their own. Doing the writing and action items in this book are critical for your success.

One thing is certain: If you are going to achieve any goal, you have to be 100 percent committed to it, believe in it, and know that it is worth the effort.

Reaching an important goal will take effort, possibly a higher level of effort than you have demonstrated in the past, but it will be well worth it.

"It's not enough that we do our best; sometimes we have to do what's required."
—Sir Winston Churchill

One payoff for reaching your goal will be a significant sense of accomplishment. This will likely have a considerable impact on your life because when you overcome numerous, often difficult, obstacles to achieve something of value, you feel exhilarated, and this feeling has long-lasting effects.

GOAL! can help you achieve any business goal. Our approach is guaranteed to be effective and, if followed faithfully, will be the launching pad for reaching all your goals.

This book is divided into two parts: Phase I consists of six chapters and Phase II contains the "30-DAY GOAL TRACK."

Phase I

In this part of the book you will learn the seven most common business goals, helping you determine which goal you want to pursue and the reasons why it is important. The next step is creating your action plan, which will detail the specifics of what you need to do in order to achieve your goal. In the remaining chapters, you will be armed with the tools to overcome any psychological barriers to success that may crop up and you will be motivated by the inspiring stories of how leaders in their fields reached the top.

Phase II: The 30-DAY GOAL TRACK

The 30-DAY GOAL TRACK will help you create new habits that will unstoppably guide you toward what you want to achieve. Human beings are creatures of habit and we are going to leverage this innate quality to help you develop habits which lead to success. What differentiates people who consistently achieve their goals from those who do not is the formation of habits that support their quests. Once you have gotten into the rhythm of doing something consistently, the odds are excellent that you will continue until you achieve your goal.

The 30-DAY GOAL TRACK is a series of daily exercises that will keep you moving toward your goal. As you proceed, the realization that you are actually going to achieve your goal will generate the enthusiasm, energy, and motivation you require to reach the finish line.

In Phase I, you will be building momentum so when you begin you will already be in motion. Read the six chapters in Phase I and do the exercises in them over the next seven days. We want you to start the specific action items towards your goal by this day next week, if not sooner.

Want vs. Should Goals

The place to start in this journey is to identify the business goal you want to tackle. If you are like most of us, there are many goals that you would like to attain. We recommend you single out the *one* goal that is most compelling to you. The one goal that you've thought a great deal about and may or may not have shared with anyone else. The one goal you *want* to pursue, not the one you think you ought to pursue.

Ask yourself if this is a goal that you are excited about. When you think about this goal do you feel energized? Is this something you really want to do, but until now have not made a priority? If you answered "yes" to these questions, you have identified the right goal.

Conversely, your goal may not be something you necessarily want to do, but something other people may be pressuring you to do. Perhaps you find your current job rewarding and wish to stay in it, while your friends or family feel you should work toward a promotion.

People who choose a goal they really want are far more likely to achieve their goal than people who choose a goal because they, or others, think they should. If your goal falls into the "should" category, or is not self-imposed, you may want to examine whether it is the right goal for you to pursue.

What Does It Take to Reach a Goal?

You need to believe in your goal wholeheartedly: believe it's worthwhile, believe that you deserve it, and believe that you can do it. These beliefs, combined with a commitment to do the work, form the key to reaching your goal.

Goals are achieved by taking an appropriate course of action over a period of time. Spending time working toward the achievement of your goal will mean less time available for other activities. For some people this creates conflicting thoughts: "Yes, I would like to get a promotion, but I really should use that extra time doing something for my family (friends, church, etc.)." Some people always put themselves last in their own lives. It's a question of balance. With the proper structure you can maximize the impact of your time and still realize your goal.

Getting to Your Goal

This flow chart is a visual representation of the broad steps you will take from first identifying your goal to achieving that goal. It shows the logical progression from inception to completion. The first step is selecting your goal.

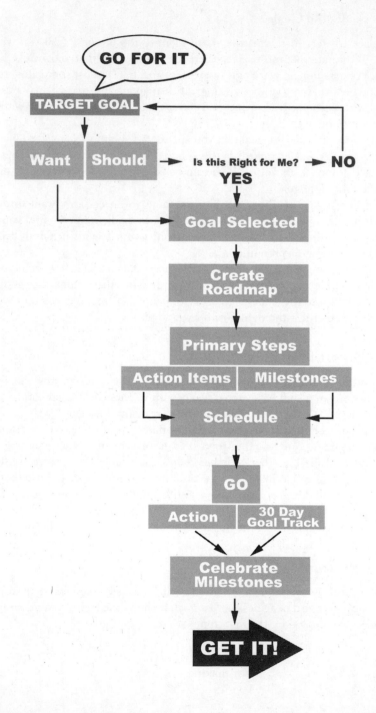

Common Business Goals

The examples presented below are some of the most common business goals people select. These examples discuss each goal in general terms, and also posit some important considerations for you to think about. We will walk you through the specifics about how to tackle your own personal goal in subsequent chapters. For now, the following examples will provide insight into how to approach your goal selection: considerations for selecting the goal, the impact the goal may have on you and others, and the potential benefits of achieving the goal. You may want to explore these issues to make sure you are focusing on the optimum goal for you.

• Start Your Own Business

Many people dream of starting their own business. Owning your own business carries with it the potential to control your destiny and create a more direct correlation between your efforts and your financial rewards.

Begin by asking yourself a number of questions. What skills do you want to leverage and what do you enjoy doing? Do you want to work alone or with a partner? Working with a partner means gaining additional perspective and provides someone with whom you can share the highs and lows. Going it alone means the responsibility for the business rests solely on your shoulders; however, you will reap 100 percent of the financial rewards.

What type of business do you want to start? Are you interested in launching a product or service that is a variation on something that already exists in the marketplace, as the founders of Google did with their Internet search engine? Or are you more inclined to introduce an entirely new product, like Procter & Gamble did with Crest White Strips, or TiVo did with the digital video recorder? You may want to take an innovative approach, like Tom Monaghan, founder of Domino's, did with pizza delivery. What had previously been viewed by his competitors as a necessary evil, Tom saw as an opportunity and turned fast delivery service into the focus of his profitable enterprise. You might also consider taking the value-added approach, like airline Jet Blue did when it initially offered amenities such as in-flight entertainment and TV on every seat without additional cost to the passenger.

You may prefer the franchise option because the bugs have been worked out and the corporate office provides operational support, product selection, and advertising. This choice may be an excellent halfway step between being employed in the corporate world and designing your own business from the ground up.

There is a unique psychological component to owning a business. Only you can determine whether you have the temperament to work without the resources of a large company or with the attendant risks that go hand in hand with owning your own business. Starting a business is like having a baby in that you are 100-percent responsible for making it successful. Long hours and deferred financial rewards can create stress on you and your family. It's possible that your desire for entrepreneurship could be satisfied by taking more of an entrepreneurial role within your current company and that this is where you should set your goal.

Starting your own business can be an exciting proposition, with a new set of challenges and potentially even greater rewards. People who own their own business say there is no greater satisfaction than knowing the success of their company was due to their own efforts.

• Get Promoted

One of the most popular goals people strive to attain is a promotion. A promotion can mean more money, more prestige, the ability to be more involved in strategic decisions, the opportunity to learn new skills, and the chance to make a greater contribution.

It is important to know, understand, and define specifically what getting a promotion will mean to you. You need to determine what the title and responsibilities are of the position you are seeking. Is it to be director of operations for a specific division at your company? If so, the responsibilities of this position will likely be clearly defined within your organization and you should learn what these are. If you are seeking this same title at another company, you will need to determine how the job is defined there. Different companies may assign broader or narrower responsibilities despite using the same title.

There is an adage in the business world that you should already be doing the job before you can be officially promoted into it. Most companies thrive by reducing risk, and the more effectively you can demonstrate to senior management that you are already performing many of the functions of the next level job, the more likely and more rapidly you will achieve that promotion. You may also want to take a more innovative approach by looking at what other companies, particularly the top-rated companies, are requiring of people in that position and incorporate those skills into your repertoire.

Being promoted will likely have an impact on your life beyond simply realizing greater financial rewards. It will undoubtedly mean more responsibility and potentially more stress and longer hours, which could affect your family and social life. Your promotion may involve managing former coworkers and, if some of them were friends, this could be an awkward situation. Higher visibility means potentially being on the "hot seat" when things don't go according to plan.

The number one reason people change jobs and pursue a promotion is because they want to make a greater impact on the organization. In a more senior role you can be the catalyst for major change, which is an exciting and energizing proposition.

• Make More Money

Most people would like to make more money. The reasons are fairly obvious: a better quality of life, being able to afford more of the things you like, and the ability to treat your family and loved ones to things they might not otherwise have access to.

First, you need to quantify what more money means. Whatever the increased amount is, it is important to define it with specificity.

There are a number of ways to approach making more money. You can find a higher paying position with another company or figure out a way to make more money in your current position. Alternatively, you may want to start your own part-time business or, if you already own a business, create multiple streams of income within that business. Reexamining your investment strategy can also lead to increased income. For example, you may decide to take a non-managerial equity position in a business or invest in real estate.

Making more money will likely require a greater commitment of time and effort on your part. More time dedicated to earning a higher income may mean less time with family and friends and less time for leisure activities. Your financial success may also impact your relationships with others.

Money is a powerful motivator and there are many ways to make more money. Effective planning and a dose of creativity can help get you there.

• Increase Productivity

If higher productivity is your goal, you have picked a goal that should pay dividends almost immediately. There are probably things you can and should do better on a consistent basis but, for whatever reason, have not done so.

Fine-tuning your efforts will have its first positive impact on you as you see the quantity and quality of your work increase. It will also have a ripple effect as those working for you and with you notice the difference and realize that the bar on performance has been raised.

There are obvious benefits to getting things done more efficiently. However, being more productive means having to reexamine everything you're doing and how you're doing it. If you've been in your position for a while, chances are there are many things you do on "automatic pilot." Doing things in a new way means changing habits, which will initially require more time and effort. Also, if you want to incorporate "best practices" into your new mode of working, this can involve learning new systems, which can involve a considerable investment in time. On the relationship side, one potential result of being more productive is that your coworkers may negatively view your raising the standard of performance.

Regarding the most important job functions that you perform, wouldn't it feel good to improve them by 10 percent, 15 percent, or 20 percent? If you're in sales, higher productivity might mean ratcheting up your presentation, which could result in better informing your clients and potentially increasing your income.

Setting your goal at higher productivity in the most important parts of your job will produce immediate rewards.

• **Change Careers**

It is very common for people to reach a point, early or later in their careers, when they question whether they would be more fulfilled doing something different. If you are considering changing careers, it is important to approach this with a great deal of thought in order to make the best choice.

There are many things to consider when contemplating a new career, but two of the most important questions you can ask yourself are:

- What do I enjoy doing?
- What am I good at?

There is power where these two things intersect. The more time you can spend doing what you enjoy, the better your quality of life will be. Leveraging what you enjoy into a new career can give you increased energy and enthusiasm for the remainder of your working life.

The impact on yourself and the people around you can be significant. If you have been demonstrably unhappy in your work, changing to a new career can provide the stimulation you have been looking for. Finding a new career that is your true calling can change your mental outlook from merely tolerating a job to doing something with a real purpose and real rewards.

A potential drawback to starting a new career is that there may be an initial dip in your earnings. However, as a rule of thumb, you should start making more money as you become more proficient in your new career. There might also be a learning curve, which for some may be daunting, while for others is exciting.

No matter where you are in life or in your career, it's never too late to change direction. Julia Child didn't start cooking until she was thirty-seven years old. Vera Wang didn't start designing wedding gowns until she was forty. Sidney Sheldon wrote his first book at age fifty-two. Anna Mary Robertson, "Grandma Moses," didn't start painting until she was in her seventies.

• **Increase Sales**

"Nothing happens until a product is sold" is more than just a saying; it's the truth. In for-profit organizations, all the research and development, new packaging, and other company efforts have no meaning if a sale isn't made.

Increasing sales helps in many ways, including these obvious two: raising cash flow and profits. But it also energizes the entire organization and motivates everyone to continue to improve the business' products or services. Of course, if your compensation is tied to sales, greater sales means more money for you personally.

If you decide to increase sales with the 80/20 rule—focusing on the 20 percent of clients that contribute 80 percent of your revenue—the rewards can be substantial. The 80/20 approach has proven effective over time because you're focusing your efforts on the areas that produce the greatest impact. The potential downside, however, is that your risks aren't being spread sufficiently. There are plenty of companies that have experienced the loss of their largest account and ended up going out of business.

You may decide to increase sales by more aggressively up-selling existing customers, either by going broader or deeper into an organization. IBM went broader and deeper into organizations by selling hardware, then software, then professional services, to different departments (e.g., finance, human resources, manufacturing). This has also been a successful strategy for many other companies. One thing to consider is while both of these techniques can dramatically increase revenue, going broader can dilute your core competency and competitive edge and going deeper can result in spending less time cultivating new clients.

There are other factors to consider if you decide to set your goal as increasing sales. You may have to work harder and longer hours. As a sales person, trying to increase sales could result in an increase in the number of times you hear "No." This additional rejection can be discouraging, yet will be worth it in the long run.

Without a doubt, increasing sales will have a positive effect on you and the organization. It can potentially increase your visibility and opportunities for promotion. Increasing sales often leads to more innovative thinking, which can be exciting and fun. The financial aspect of increasing sales, especially if it's linked to your compensation, can be very rewarding.

• Develop a High Performance Team

Something that most managers strive for is developing a team that maximizes its performance over both the short and long term. It is a goal that will bring the team closer together as a unit, increase pride in the output of the team, and significantly raise the visibility of the team within the organization.

If this is a goal you have chosen to address, there are a number of things that you should consider as you approach the planning stage of the goal. Like a head coach of a football or basketball team, one of the keys to building a high performance team is integrating the individual strengths of the team members into a cohesive unit. This involves an assessment by you of each team member's strengths and weaknesses and how these strengths can best be deployed to help reach the team's overall goals. You can determine what each team member does best by both observing their work and by asking them what they get the greatest enjoyment from doing and what they believe they do best.

As a manager in pursuit of this goal, you will also want to balance the leveraging of each person's strength with the need to try to develop those areas in which the individual may need improvement. Focus on letting people on the team do what they do best, but do this in conjunction with consistent, ongoing training.

Not every team member will embrace your desire for higher performance. They may view it as requiring more effort on their part and therefore as a negative. This in turn will require more energy from you to make sure that everyone's on board and motivated to give their best. Change is never easy and is not always instantaneous. It sometimes requires two steps forward and one step back.

Building a high performance team is also contingent upon making sure that everyone understands the goals and objectives for the team, and by measuring on a regular basis how the team is performing in regard to goals.

* * *

Outside the realm of these common business goals is the category of humanitarian goals. While your company may have programs dedicated to corporate social responsibility, you may still want to make a contribution on your own. If you have the desire to volunteer, yet have never found the time to do so, consider approaching humanitarian efforts as you would any other goal.

Your natural instinct may be to gravitate towards the cause you are most passionate about. However, depending on that organization's specific needs, your talents may be better served in a charity that is lower on your priority list, but in greater need of your specific abilities. It will also be important for you to determine how you want to contribute. Do you want to be on the frontlines with the recipients, perhaps doing something like serving meals to those in need, or would you rather do administrative work such as fund-raising? In addition, ask yourself what level of commitment you are willing to make. Would you rather commit to the completion of a specific project, like a charity drive, or do you want an ongoing commitment with a specified number of hours each month?

A humanitarian goal is a worthwhile endeavor which will improve the quality of your life as well as those you are helping. The key is to take a balanced approach—know what you can comfortably give and how that will mesh with the organization's needs.

Define Your Goal

We're going to ask you to think about your goal only in a positive way. Approach your goal based on all the reasons it *can* be done. For now, put aside whatever doubts you may have, as we will address those later. Your new reality is that you can accomplish your goal. Starting now, believe that you can do it.

"Change your thoughts and you change your world."
                                                                —Norman Vincent Peale

As you define your goal, specificity will be key. For example, if you decide your goal is to make more money, how much more? You can define this in either a percentage or dollar amount, whichever you prefer. The important thing is to be specific about what you are going after.

Take a moment to consider what it is that you want to achieve:

1. Write down your goal.
Be specific. For example, if your goal is to start your own business, what type of

business will it be? The more specific you can be, the better your ability to create a plan to get you there.

_____

_____

Now that you have selected your goal, ask yourself why this goal is important to you. For example, Jordan is a brand manager for a large consumer packaged goods company. His goal is to introduce a new product and the following are the reasons he wants to do this:

- "If my product launch is successful, it will have a positive effect on the marketplace."
- "New product introductions get lots of attention, which will give me greater visibility within my company."
- "I'll get more respect from my peers."

Think through your goal so that you know *why* you want to achieve it. The "why" is your motivation and it is critical to achieving your goal. In the above example, Jordan is motivated by three things. It doesn't matter how many motivating factors you have; what matters is that you know what they are. These factors will help sustain you should you feel the desire to quit.

2. List your motivations for wanting to achieve your goal.

_____

_____

_____

_____

Now let's take things to a deeper level. What are your feelings associated with achieving your goal?

Continuing with Jordan's example, here are the feelings (in bold) he believes he'll have once he reaches his goal:

- "If the marketplace benefits from my new product, I'll have more **self-confidence**, knowing I was able to address an important need."
- "Higher visibility means more opportunities, which for me is **exciting**."

- "By gaining the respect of my peers, I will be more **secure** while contributing my thoughts and ideas in meetings."

Notice how his feelings link to each one of his motivations. Why is it important to know the feelings involved in reaching your goal? You need to know your goal intimately. When you know what you want—how it looks and how it feels—then you can begin to go after it.

3. Describe how you will feel when you reach your goal.
Give this response very careful thought. Each feeling should link to its corresponding motivation you listed on number 2.

_____

_____

_____

_____

* * *

Clearly, achieving your goal will require a positive mind-set. The following example illustrates the importance of this.

Mark

Mark is an intelligent 46-year-old. He earned his masters and doctorate in biogenetics from a prestigious university. He has worked as a research scientist with the same company for many years and has been successful in his career. Unfortunately, he found himself becoming too comfortable in his current position and was getting bored. Mark wanted to take on new challenges and make a greater contribution. He wanted to move up in the organization.

His motivations and feelings for wanting a promotion included:

- "I want to take on a new challenge because it will be energizing, fun, and I can make a bigger impact."
- "I love mentoring and want to spend more time doing that. Being promoted will give me a larger team and that will enable me to spend more time helping people."
- "I'll make more money, which means I'll be able to splurge, now and then, on myself and my family."

Here is what Mark listed for the three items above:

Goal: Promotion to Senior Scientist.
Motivations: New challenges, more mentoring opportunities, bigger salary.
Feelings: Making a greater impact will make my work feel more meaningful. Taking on new challenges will be energizing and fun. Mentoring is enjoyable. More money will allow me the pleasure of giving more to myself and my family.

The "Knowing-Doing Gap"

Mark knew that the key to getting promoted was to achieve greater visibility within his company. This could be done by presenting to other scientists at the monthly journal clubs. Before making any presentations, Mark would have to read various scientific journals and then present the findings.

Mark knew his goal, and he knew this was an important step toward obtaining it; he just wasn't doing it. This is called "the knowing-doing gap." In order to bridge that gap, Mark had to identify what was holding him back.

Identifying and Overcoming the Hurdle

In many ways, Mark is a disciplined person in his life and career. He earned a Ph.D. from Johns Hopkins University, he works out regularly, and he sets aside time on a weekly basis for activities with his children.

With our help, Mark identified the main reason he was not moving forward—his negative thought patterns:

- "I can't distinguish myself in front of such intelligent people [the other scientists]."
- "If I do get promoted, my raise won't offset the additional stress."
- "With more responsibilities, I will have less time with my family."

These were paralyzing thoughts for him, but were they true?

He evaluated each of these statements and realized they were not valid. His thoughts were based in fear—not reality. He developed the following replacement thoughts:

- "Even though my colleagues are intelligent, there are things they can learn from me."
- "I'm the one in control of my stress and I can manage that."
- "With more responsibilities come more resources, so I can still maintain a good work/life balance."

With these positive thoughts, he started a new "internal dialogue," one that supported him toward achieving his goal. In a short period of time, Mark was promoted.

* * *

Did you hear something of yourself in Mark's negative thoughts? We all engage in an internal dialogue. Some people accept negative thoughts without questioning where they originated or without challenging their validity.

Negative thoughts can be based in fear, doubt, guilt, or discouragement—or a combination of any of these. Sometimes they come from other people (parents, coworkers, friends, etc.) who may have convinced you that certain things were beyond your abilities. By continuing this negative self-talk, you are perpetuating the myth other people have tried to instill in you.

Many years ago, people thought that running a four-minute mile was physically impossible, that the human body could not sustain the required speed over that distance. At some point, people began to challenge this notion, believing that it might be possible. Once the negative thought barrier was broken, tens and then hundreds of runners subsequently broke this four-minute mile physical "barrier." (In Chapter Six, we will discuss this particular achievement in greater detail.)

Your mind is the most powerful ally you have. It can spur you on to achieve things you thought were not possible. The fuel for this forward movement is positive thinking. It will sustain you during those times when you have doubts about your ability to achieve the goal.

"If you think you can do a thing or think you can't do a thing, you're right."
—Henry Ford

4. List your thoughts on why you believe you can't achieve or shouldn't pursue your goal.
Even the most positive people have doubts, and it's likely that you have some as well. Even if these doubts seem small or insignificant, list them here so that they can be addressed.

_____

_____

_____

_____

5. Write down corresponding positive replacement thoughts.
Now replace each of these negative thoughts with a positive one. This is very important because these positive thoughts will carry you over the hurdles that negative thoughts create.

_____

_____

_____

_____

These positive thoughts may not be easy for you to accept at this point. They may seem superficial or too much to hope for. However, in a short while, the exercises in this book will make it easier for you to "own" these thoughts.

* * *

To sum up your progress thus far: You have identified your goal and your motivations and feelings around attaining this goal, and your negative thoughts have been replaced with positive ones. These are important initial steps toward achieving your goal. You have now created momentum.

"The beginning is the most important part of the work."

—Plato

Action Items   **Check When Done**

Identify your goal.   ☐

List your motivations and feelings concerning your goal.   ☐
(Place lists where you will see them every day.)

Replace negative thoughts with positive ones.   ☐
(Place list where you can read it and repeat these positive
thoughts to yourself every day.)

Commit to start working on your goal by this day next   ☐
week, if not sooner.

CHAPTER TWO
Create the Road Map

Breaking Down Your Goal

To some people, evaluating a goal and identifying what needs to be done in order to accomplish that goal can seem overwhelming. Breaking down your goal into manageable steps creates order, reduces stress, and allows you to tackle the overall goal in smaller pieces. Importantly, it provides a beginning point, as many well-intentioned people just don't know where to start.

In this chapter, we will introduce a 4-Step Goal Planning Worksheet to help you reach your goal (an online version of the worksheet is available at www.GoalThere.com). Briefly, the four steps are: 1) list the Primary Steps you must take to achieve your goal, 2) assign them to the month they should occur, 3) break down your Primary Steps into individual Action Items, and 4) schedule the specific day and time you will work on each Action Item. Completing the Goal Planning Worksheet will take a fair amount of time and effort, as it is the platform for your goal attainment.

At this point you already know what your goal is and why it's important to you. Now you need to determine the specific course of action required to achieve the goal and the time frame involved. While some people may be very clear about the steps necessary to achieve their goal, others may not be. If you are not certain about what needs to be done, do some research. You can also consult professionals in the area of your goal or speak with friends and colleagues who may have accomplished what you are setting out to do.

Once you have identified the appropriate course of action and determined when you want to complete your goal, the key will be consistency. Consistently doing each action in a specified time frame keeps you moving forward. Staying focused on each successive activity will create a domino effect until you eventually reach your goal.

Without question, achieving your goal will require discipline. You may not think of yourself as a highly disciplined person, but in many ways you already are. Any activity that you do on a consistent basis is a pattern of behavior and demonstrates a degree of discipline. There are probably many things you currently do in a disciplined way; for example, preparing weekly management reports. We are going to tap into the discipline you already demonstrate in certain areas of your professional life and apply it to the goal achievement process you are about to undertake.

Every goal involves a number of discreet steps. Before you go through the exercise of listing the various steps of your goal, think about the timing of your goal. If your goal doesn't have a specific date, assign it an arbitrary, but realistic one. When determining a date for your goal, pick one that will be appropriately aggressive, yet attainable. Set an end date that will require consistent effort on your part.

Goal Date: By when (month/year) do you want to accomplish your goal? __ / __

This Goal Date, just like a deadline at work, will determine when things need to be done. Once you have identified the actual steps to take you may have to change your Goal Date slightly to coincide with them. Now that you have decided on your Goal Date, determine what specific steps need to be done. Every goal has a number of Primary Steps. This number will vary based on the complexity of your project. Some of the steps may be sequential or concurrent depending on the goal.

Continuing with the example of the most common business goals from Chapter One, this is how you would identify the Primary Steps.

Start Your Own Business in One Year

Assume that you have been a CPA in an accounting firm for the past five years and decide to fulfill your life-long dream by starting your own company. What are some of the main components, or Primary Steps, you will need to take in order to launch your business? These steps will probably include renting office space, hiring employees, getting new clients, developing a niche in the marketplace, and advertising your services.

Get Promoted in Three Months

Suppose you are a senior brand manager at a retail company and want to be promoted to director of marketing. The company you work for typically promotes people to the director level once they have grown a brand, effectively managed a team, introduced new products, and have shown initiative outside of their functional area. In this case, these benchmarks would serve as your Primary Steps.

Make More Money (15 Percent) in Six Months

In your current position, the maximum bonus you can earn is 25 percent, but you have been averaging only 10 percent. Your goal is to earn the maximum bonus, which is an increase of 15 percent. Maximum bonuses are paid out when there is a significant increase in the profitability of your product. Your Primary Steps might be reducing manufacturing costs, negotiating a new contract with your advertising agency, identifying new strategic partners with whom to co-market your products, working with product development to use lower-cost ingredients, and increasing distribution.

Increase Productivity in Thirty Days

While you have been effective in your current role, more is being asked of you and you need to increase your productivity. You think of how you have been spending your time and decide these will be your Primary Steps: run your meetings with tighter agendas, create more accountability with your project team, set clearer goals and priorities, measure progress more frequently, and incorporate a more aggressive reward system for your team.

Change Careers

After being successful in your current career, you decide it's time for a change. You are not sure what you want to do but know that you want to go in a new direction. The Primary Steps could be to determine what you want to do, identify what skill set is needed and what gaps you need to fill, shore up skills needed, network with others who are currently doing this job, and attend seminars to learn more about the industry.

Increase Sales

As a software sales person, you have been successful but believe you could be even more aggressive. Higher sales will translate to more money, higher visibility, and more perks. The Primary Steps you have identified are to target a new vertical industry, expand the channels in your market, learn more about your competitors to strengthen your sales presentation, focus your efforts on the high-potential accounts (the 80/20 rule), and up-sell to existing customers.

Develop a High Performance Team

As the director of a critical department, you want to develop your team to their fullest extent. Your plan includes the following Primary Steps: determine what motivates each member of your team to incentivize them to their highest performance, integrate individual strengths into a cohesive unit, organize off-site team bonding activities, align the corporate goals with those of your team and communicate how they are linked, and recognize your team's achievements verbally and monetarily.

* * *

The best way to identify your Primary Steps is to start thinking of the main components of your goal. It is not necessary to put them in order at this point, just start listing them.

Here are some example goals and their Primary Steps:

Goal: Develop a Business Plan in Three Months

Primary Step #1 Write executive summary (mission statement, overall goals).
Primary Step #2 SWOT analysis (strengths, weaknesses, opportunities, threats).
Primary Step #3 Write company description (nature of business and prospects for success).
Primary Step #4 Evaluate organization and management (who does what?).
Primary Step #5 Assess financial situation (profit, ROI, etc.).

Goal: Name a New Product in Thirty Days

Primary Step #1 Create a list of adjectives that describe the product.
Primary Step #2 Develop creative brief around the product.
Primary Step #3 Get senior management approval.
Primary Step #4 Conduct a legal name search and then trademark name.
Primary Step #5 Brainstorm with coworkers.

Goal: Get an MBA in Two Years

Primary Step #1 Identify and apply to appropriate schools.
Primary Step #2 Calculate various costs associated with obtaining the degree.
Primary Step #3 Consider alternative sources of financing.
Primary Step #4 Develop your course road map.
Primary Step #5 Prepare and take GMAT.

The steps provided for each goal are not meant to be all-inclusive. Your goal may have more or fewer Primary Steps.

The 4-Step Goal Planning Worksheet

Step 1: List Primary Steps

Identify the steps that need to be taken. What Primary Steps do you need to take to accomplish your goal? These do not need to be put in order at this point.

Primary Step #1_____
Primary Step #2_____
Primary Step #3_____
Primary Step #4_____
Primary Step #5_____

Now that you have identified the Primary Steps of your goal, you have completed Step 1 in the Goal Planning Worksheet. There are four steps to completing the worksheet: Listing your Primary Steps; entering those steps in the month they should occur; breaking down the steps into individual Action Items; and then scheduling a day and time when you will work on your Action Items.

Here is an example of how Primary Step #3 from the goal "Develop a Business Plan in Three Months" will look when it is completed:

Develop a Business Plan
Goal Planning Worksheet
Month One

Primary Step	Action Items	Week #	Day & Time
Write Company Description	Identify Target Market	3	Tu: 2–4 PM
	List Primary Success Factors	4	M & W: 1–3 PM
	Products/Services Sold	2	Th: 8–10 AM
	Describe Nature of Business	1	F: 8–9:30 AM

This format will be followed for each Primary Step in the appropriate month leading up to completion of your goal. Review your Primary Steps and determine in what month they need to be performed. Use your Goal Date to help you plan. The sequence of events may be important, so spend the time necessary to think this through. What logically should happen first, second, third, etc. for the project to move forward to completion?

Use the following worksheet and, for now, enter only the Primary Steps which you just identified. The Action Items, Week #, and Day & Time columns will be completed later in the chapter. The Primary Steps should be entered in the month they need to take place. For example, if your Primary Step #3 should take place during the first month of your goal, then list that step on the worksheet entitled "Month One." We have provided three months of worksheets. If your goal takes longer, make additional copies.

Step 2: Take your previously determined Primary Steps and write them on the Goal Planning Worksheet below.
Use your Goal Date to determine in what months they should occur.

Goal Planning Worksheet
(available at www.GoalThere.com)
Month One

Primary Step	Action Items	Week #	Day & Time
_____	_____	_____	_____
	_____	_____	_____
	_____	_____	_____
	_____	_____	_____
_____	_____	_____	_____
	_____	_____	_____
	_____	_____	_____
_____	_____	_____	_____
	_____	_____	_____
	_____	_____	_____
	_____	_____	_____

Goal Planning Worksheet
(available at www.GoalThere.com)
Month Two

Primary Step	Action Items	Week #	Day & Time
_____	_____	_____	_____
	_____	_____	_____

_____   _____   _____

_____   _____   _____

_____   _____   _____

_____   _____

_____   _____   _____

_____   _____   _____

_____   _____   _____

_____   _____   _____

_____   _____

_____   _____   _____

_____   _____   _____

_____   _____   _____

Goal Planning Worksheet
(available at www.GoalThere.com)
Month Three

Primary Step	Action Items	Week #	Day & Time
_____	_____	_____	_____
	_____	_____	_____
	_____	_____	_____
	_____	_____	_____
_____	_____	_____	_____
	_____	_____	_____
	_____	_____	_____
	_____	_____	_____
_____	_____	_____	_____
	_____	_____	_____
	_____	_____	_____
	_____	_____	_____

The next step in the process is to convert each of your Primary Steps into specific Action Items. Each Primary Step might have multiple Action Items associated with it.

Step 3: Break down your Primary Steps into individual Action Items.
For example, in the "Develop a Business Plan" goal, the Primary Step "Write Company Description" has the following Action Items:

Primary Step	Action Items	Week #	Day & Time
Write Company Description	Identify Target Market	_____	_____
	List Primary Success Factors	_____	_____
	Products/Services Sold	_____	_____
	Describe Nature of Business	_____	_____

Now use the Goal Planning Worksheet on the preceding pages to break down your Primary Steps into individual Action Items.

Step 4 (Final Step): Schedule day and time for each action item.
The planning is now at its most specific phase. Daily activities need to be planned and times assigned within those days for the activities to occur.

Now that your Primary Steps have been assigned to the appropriate month and broken down into Action Items, the next thing you need to do is schedule what day and time within each week you will work on the activity. Continuing with our business plan example, here is an example of how the scheduling will look:

Primary Step	Action Items	Week #	Day & Time
Write Company Description	Identify Target Market	3	Tu: 2–4 PM
	List Primary Success Factors	4	M & W: 1–3 PM
	Products/Services Sold	2	Th: 8–10 AM
	Describe Nature of Business	1	F: 8–9:30 AM

Now use the Goal Planning Worksheet to enter the specific day and time within each week that you will be working on your Action Items. Remember that consistent activity will get you into the habit of attaining what is important to you, so make sure you are working towards your goal several times a week.

Once the Goal Planning Worksheet has been completed, take your scheduled Actions Items and enter the day and time as appointments into your calendar, scheduling them for next week, if not sooner. Mark each appointment as "Important." By making a commitment to start by at least next week, you will be within days of acting toward your goal.

* * *

Most people have systems for scheduling and keeping appointments. Whether you use a paper calendar, Microsoft Outlook, a PDA, or a cell phone, determine if it is indeed working for you. It is important that you use a system that will keep you on track. Achieving your goal means keeping your scheduled appointments and that requires diligence.

* * *

Your goal is now broken down into manageable pieces and scheduled accordingly. While some of you may be energized that you now have a plan, others may feel overwhelmed by looking at everything that needs to be done. In the aggregate it may look like a lot of work, but the reality is that it will be done over time and feel quite manageable.

The Comfort Zone

In reaching your goal you may be required to do things that you are unaccustomed to doing and which may take you outside of your comfort zone. The comfort zone is comprised of all the things we normally do and which therefore feel "comfortable." New experiences typically take us outside our comfort zone and the plan you have created for your goal may fall into this category. For example, your goal may be to speak at a large conference and the thought of this may give rise to fear and anxiety. When the comfort zone is at odds with what we need to do to realize our goal, the tendency may be to forget about it. The fact that you are aspiring to achieve a goal that might be outside your comfort zone is an indication that you are ready to take that leap. This "zone" is malleable and will expand as much as you require it to. As unnerving as it may be, once you get into the rhythm of doing something new, your comfort zone will adjust to allow for it.

"I believe that one of life's greatest risks is never daring to risk."
—Oprah Winfrey

Accountability Partner

Many people fall short of their goal because they do not have an accountability piece built into the plan. Accountability is important because it can help keep you on track. It can be easy to make an excuse to yourself, but it is much more difficult when you have to be accountable to another person.

Because too many of us have difficulty keeping commitments to ourselves, we recommend incorporating the assistance of another person. This means identifying someone who can be your accountability partner. It doesn't matter whether it is a friend, spouse, family member, or coworker; what matters is that this individual will be supportive and hold you accountable.

If you believe you can benefit from an Accountability Partner, identify who that person will be. Let the person know you will be contacting him or her on a monthly basis to provide an update on how you are doing against plan.

Course Correction

As you monitor your progress towards achieving your goal, it is possible that you might not see the progress you had hoped for. If you are doing the work and not getting the results you expected, make changes—either in the activities themselves or in their order. Flexibility is important and there may be many ways to get to your goal. Look upon less-than-expected results as information which can guide you to the most appropriate course of action. Act decisively when it is time to make a change.

If you are attempting a goal that you have tried to achieve in the past, think back to what caused you to get off track. There are many things in life that can interfere with your progress—product recall, business travel, special events, etc.

When we fall behind schedule it is human nature to castigate ourselves. We may feel that we have let ourselves and others down.

It's usually at this point—when people feel disappointed in themselves—that they "check out." They label themselves as procrastinators or a host of other things and give up.

At some point they may attempt the goal again. Often, the same cycle occurs— a good start, followed by a concerted effort, followed by an interruption, followed by a disappointment, resulting in abandonment of the goal.

People who regularly achieve goals understand that there is an ebb and flow to reaching a goal. When they get off track, they don't berate themselves, they just get back on track as soon as possible.

An Example of Course Correction
Julia Stewart, CEO of IHOP

Successful executives can usually point to at least one example of course correction in their careers. In the case of Julia Stewart, hers is a very interesting story.

Julia had successfully risen through the marketing ranks at companies like Burger King and Black Angus before reaching the level of vice president of operations at Taco Bell. Julia's ultimate goal was to be CEO of a large corporation. With that in mind, she left Taco Bell and joined Applebee's as president of their Domestic Division. She reported directly to the CEO, Lloyd Hill, and made her CEO career ambitions known. The two had discussed the possibility of her rise to the job within a couple of years, assuming she had demonstrated the necessary capabilities. Under her leadership, Applebee's sales grew significantly.

"I went into his [CEO Lloyd Hill's] office one day, and said, 'It's been three years. It's time,'" she remembers. "He said, 'Nah, I don't think so.' And I said, 'Then it was probably best to leave.'"

Julia believed she had been on course to become Applebee's CEO and, when she realized it wasn't going to happen, she knew she needed to change course. Leaving Applebee's allowed her to dedicate herself to pursuing a new opportunity.

In December 2001, Stewart landed the president and COO job at IHOP Corporation and, importantly, was promoted to CEO within a few months.

Had she remained at Applebee's, mostly likely, she would still be waiting for the CEO job. By making that important course correction, she was able to reach her ultimate goal.

An interesting footnote is that Julia engineered the IHOP purchase of Applebee's in 2007.

* * *

The best thing you can do if you are off track is to identify what needs to be done to get back on course and start again.

Reaching Milestones

Milestones are the significant achievements you realize along the way. They mark the progress you are making and should be acknowledged, as they confirm you are getting closer to your ultimate goal. A logical approach to identifying your milestones is to determine which significant points in the development of your goal should be recognized. For example, if your sales goal is $1,000,000, a milestone might be when you reach $250,000. Set your milestones appropriately so that they represent significant progress. It is important to have at least three milestones to measure your progress and keep yourself motivated.

Many people reach their goal by focusing on each successive milestone. Milestones should be acknowledged and celebrated, as they are the recognition of an achievement.

What will your milestones be and when will you achieve them?

_____

_____

_____

How will you celebrate when you reach each milestone? Each milestone could have a different reward attached to it (e.g., a special purchase, a weekend getaway). Make sure that the celebration does not conflict with your goal.

_____

_____

_____

Now enter each milestone date and the associated celebration date in your calendar. When you take the time to plan your day, you are creating a habit that makes the attainment of each goal much easier.

* * *

Take a moment to reflect on how far you have come already. You have taken some significant steps in achieving your goal. By creating a workable plan and establishing specific time periods to accomplish those discreet activities, you are well on your way to successfully attaining your goal.

Action Items   Check When Done

Goal Date established. ☐

Primary Steps for accomplishing goal listed and broken down into daily Actions Items. ☐

Daily Action Items scheduled in your calendar. ☐

Milestones and their celebrations scheduled in your calendar. ☐

If needed, Accountability Partner contacted. ☐

CHAPTER THREE
See It, Make It Real

The mind is very powerful and we are going to put that power to work. Specifically, we are going to call upon the power of your subconscious to repeatedly deliver a message of how your success will look and feel to you. What the mind can visualize can be achieved, and you are going to set your mind's eye on what success looks like and, in doing so, what will help bring it about.

The subconscious accepts what you tell it and brings it into reality. If you plant thoughts and images of success in your subconscious, your brain will find ways to make success happen.

When you look at a photo of people relaxing on a Caribbean beach, it may conjure up the warmth of the sand, the feel of the sun on your face, the taste of the salt air, and a feeling of relaxation. All this happens in an instant and impacts you on an emotional level.

Advertisers have long known the value of linking pictures with words in order to reinforce their message. They look for powerful motivating images that will drive human behavior. Importantly, they understand that a key motivation is showing the end result. Fitness clubs typically advertise using pictures of people whose bodies are already in great shape because showing the end result (a great body) is a strong motivator in getting people to join health clubs. Advertisers rely on decades of research to tap into your emotions and get you to act as they desire.

We are going to use a similar strategy to help motivate you to take action toward the achievement of your goal. In effect, the goal you have written down is your "advertising copy" and now we are going to create visuals that will inspire action toward your goal.

The start of every vision begins with the end in mind. The following are three inspiring examples of how visualization can lead to extraordinary results.

Jack Nicklaus, Professional Golfer

"First I 'see' the ball where I want it to finish, nice and white and sitting up high on the bright green grass. Then the scene quickly changes, and I 'see' the ball going there: its path, trajectory, and shape, even its behavior on landing. Then there's a sort of fade-out, and the next scene shows me making the kind of swing that will turn the previous images into reality."

—Jack Nicklaus

Bill Gates, Co-founder of Microsoft Corporation

"When my friend Paul Allen and I started Microsoft thirty years ago, we had a vision of 'a computer on every desk and in every home,' which probably sounded a little too optimistic at a time when most computers were the size of refrigerators. But we believed that personal computers would change the world. And they have."

—Bill Gates

Jim Carrey, Comic and Actor

Jim Carrey has often told the story about how important visualization has been in his life. Specifically, in 1991, while he was a struggling comedian, he used to drive up to Mulholland Drive in Los Angeles to overlook the spectacular Hollywood view. On one of these trips, he wrote himself a check for $10 million and post-dated it Thanksgiving, 1995. The check was for "acting services rendered" and he kept it in his wallet as a visual reminder. Jim actually received the $10 million six months before the 1995 check date.

"Since I was a little kid, I've been visualizing my life."

—Jim Carrey

Your Vision

Every vision begins with the end in mind. Think about how it will "look" at the completion of your goal—when your new product is the market leader, when you have started your new business, when you have been promoted to vice president, when you've reached your multimillion dollar sales goal. Whatever your goal is, it has an end point and it's important to focus on this at a sensory level. Images are a surefire way to do this.

For example, your goal might be to become CEO of a company. Find a picture of a corner office and a conference room and picture yourself at these locations. Picture yourself leading an important meeting in the conference room, strategizing with a vice president in your office, or giving an interview to *FORTUNE* magazine. The important thing is to find images and other sensory triggers that connect you with your goal on an emotional level.

One way to organize these images is to create a "vision board"—a collage of pictures representing what your goal looks like. Some of you may be thinking that discussing a vision board is out of place in a business book. However, there are common elements in all goal achievement, whether the goal is personal or professional. The ability to visualize your goal is one of these common elements. Bill Gates, John F. Kennedy, and Walt Disney are examples of people who used visualization to reach their goals.

Best-selling author John Assaraf has used the power of visualization to create four multimillion dollar companies. As a business consultant, he lectures across the country about the effectiveness of visualization.

Before John was the success he is today, he decided to represent with pictures some of the materialistic things he wanted to achieve in his life. He cut out pictures of a house, a car, and a number of other things he wanted, and he put them together on a vision board. Every day, for two to three minutes, he would close his eyes and see himself having his dream car, his dream house, and a specific amount of money in the bank.

Years later, after he had achieved great success, his young son came across the vision boards, which had been boxed up for many years. He asked John what they were and, in the course of explaining the concept, John saw one particular photo on the vision board and had an amazing revelation. Unbeknownst to him, John realized that the dream house on one of his vision boards was in fact the home he now owned and had been living in for a year! John had no idea he was living in the same house he had spent minutes every day dreaming about years before.

Whatever images you choose, it is important to display them so that you can experience them on a daily basis. Jim Carrey looked at the $10 million check in his wallet on a regular basis until that representation became a reality.

At this point, let's focus on your goal and how it looks to you. Picture what your goal is and how you will experience it.

1. What visuals are parts of your goal?

_____

_____

_____

_____

_____

Creating Your Visuals

The Internet, books, and magazines can be excellent sources for images. At this point, we would like you to select an image for each item you listed above in number 1. After you have done this, place the images in such a way that you will see them daily. At some point during each day, concentrate for two minutes on how it "feels" to have reached your goal. Be as specific as possible, including the people who are likely to be a part of your success and the setting.

Experience It

When visualizing, it's important to bring together all the senses to create an actual experience. Experiencing your goal is a step beyond just picturing it. It's how it feels *today,* not how it will feel in the future.

When your subconscious experiences or "feels" something, it believes it is real and starts working towards making it tangible.

For example, maybe you are thinking about purchasing a BMW and start noticing more of these cars on the road. There aren't more of them around, you are just more aware of them. Your subconscious has started working to make your goal more tangible and it does this by raising your goal to a more conscious level. The more you focus on something the greater your awareness is, the stronger your feelings are, and the closer you come to realizing your goal.

Dr. Charles Garfield, best-selling author of *Peak Performers* and notable expert on high-achieving athletes, business leaders, and astronauts, observes:

"Peak performers develop powerful mental images of the behavior that will lead to the desired results. They see in their mind's eye the result they want, and the actions leading to it.

"I've discovered that numerous peak performers use the skill of mental rehearsal of visualization. They mentally run through important events before they happen."

This is why it is important for you to "experience" your goal. Here is how, in broad strokes, your business goal could be experienced: Think of yourself as the CEO of a company. You start the morning by addressing the entire company regarding your vision for the future. Following that meeting, you spend two hours being interviewed by *FORTUNE* magazine for a cover story. Later in the day, you have the pleasure of promoting someone to vice president. At the end of the day, from your beautiful corner office, you are on a conference call about acquiring another company.

In all likelihood, you have started to experience the powerful emotion of reaching this goal. The good energy you just created will propel you toward your goal.

* * *

2. List at least three examples of how you are currently experiencing your goal. Remember that you are experiencing it in the present: how it looks and feels to you today. For example, if your goal is to manage the London office of your advertising agency, one of your experiences could be: "Doing business in London is exciting and I love learning the culture!"

_____

_____

_____

_____

Affirmations

Most people are familiar with affirmations, those daily positive statements we say to ourselves. Affirmations are really just statements that condition you for success.

The experiences you have written down in number 2 above can serve as these positive statements. Say them slowly enough so that you focus on the message.

Start your day by conditioning your mind, affirming your goal, and carrying that energy with you throughout the day. This energy will keep you motivated and help you attract what you are looking to achieve. This is such a critical component to goal achievement that it should be scheduled so that you practice it daily.

Just as breaking down your goal in the previous chapter helped make it seem more manageable, visualizing the end result will make it seem more real. The exercises you have completed in these first three chapters have created the foundation for your ultimate success. The next three chapters are designed to provide further impetus along the road to your goal.

Action Items   Check When Done

Select visuals that represent your goal and place them where you will see them daily   ☐

Photocopy or cut out your list of how you are experiencing your goal (number 2 above) and repeat these as affirmations every day   ☐

CHAPTER FOUR
Maintain Momentum

Most people have the best of intentions when they begin a project. Unfortunately, many of those projects are left unfinished. Since you know yourself better than anyone else, where are you likely to stumble in the course of achieving your goal? Is it difficult to get started? Is it hard to stay on track or hard to continue when you are close to the finish line? If you know where you are likely to experience hurdles, now is the time to start planning the solutions to them.

There are reasons we allow things to intrude on our ability to make progress toward reaching our goal. Sometimes these are legitimate, things but frequently they are a result of psychological barriers of our own making. We will examine the common reasons barriers are created and consider strategies for overcoming them. We will concentrate on four areas: building self-esteem, conquering procrastination, moving past frustrations, and regaining motivation.

By addressing these areas early on, you will be well positioned to accomplish your goal. There is great satisfaction derived from knowing that once you start something, you will finish it.

Building Self-Esteem

People with self-esteem have harnessed one of the strongest forces in the universe. Self-esteem creates happiness, loving relationships, and the energy to be extremely productive. It gives you the power to work through issues that may crop up during the course of attaining your goal. Because self-esteem is so important, we want to address issues you may have with your self-esteem, issues that might be holding you back from achieving your goal:

• **Believe you can do it.**

Somewhere along the way you may have told yourself, or others may have told you, that you are limited in what you can achieve. They may have implied that you do not have the intellectual capacity required to accomplish a goal or the stick-to-itiveness or the ability to be resourceful. Unfortunately, many people accept a limiting view of themselves versus what they are capable of. They are convinced they do not have what it takes to be successful.

Their evidence for this may be based on past results. Perhaps you have tried to be successful in some area in the past and didn't get the outcome you desired. The reason for that could have been that you just didn't have the right resources or approach. When you learn from experiences that didn't work, you are that much closer to being successful.

Thomas Edison, Inventor

Thomas Edison is an example of someone who learned from what didn't work in the past. Edison had thousands of negative outcomes to his experiments, outcomes which he viewed as valuable information: "I have not failed. I've just found 10,000 ways that won't work."

Edison did not let unfavorable outcomes deter him from moving forward. He eventually invented the light bulb, the phonograph, and the motion picture. In his lifetime he developed 1,000 patents.

You can draw upon your past experience—even if it did not have the outcome you wanted—to achieve your goal. You have the choice to look on past results as inhibitors to future success or as a springboard to achieving what you want.

How you choose to look at your abilities is of paramount importance. For example, you may not believe that you have the ability to be persistent. However, consider that you learned to walk after falling down numerous times. Persistence is like a muscle and it needs to be exercised. If you have not been practicing persistence, clearly you need to change this. You can do this by requiring more from yourself than you have in the past. Knowing you have the ability to be persistent and combining that with your motivation for your goal will help you stick to it.

To achieve your goal, all you need to do are the right things in the right sequence. Even someone like Edison, who is universally acknowledged as extremely intelligent, emphasized the importance of hard work over natural intelligence. His famous quote, *"Genius is one percent inspiration, ninety-nine percent perspiration,"* says it all.

• **Release guilt.**

The advantage of achieving your goal is clear: It will enrich your life and is therefore a worthwhile endeavor. Say, for example, your goal is to transition out of sales and go into marketing. This move will require a greater time commitment on your part. It's something you really want to do; however, you may tell yourself that this will mean less time with your family. The irony is that by investing in yourself you enrich other relationships. By living a more fulfilled life, you are in a better position to make greater contributions to the lives of others.

J.K. Rowling, Successful Author

J.K. Rowling is an amazing success story, having sold more than a quarter-billion books from her Harry Potter series of novels.

Before she achieved success, she was a divorced mother raising a three-month-old daughter. Rowling suffered from bouts of depression and was in dire financial straits. She was living on a modest income and couldn't even afford a secondhand typewriter. Many people in similar circumstances would have concentrated on getting a second job for additional income. She could have easily told herself, "I shouldn't be spending time writing a fantasy novel. I should be thinking of ways to bring in more money."

However, Rowling was focused on her dream of becoming a writer. As it turned out, because of the investment she made in herself she has inspired millions of children to read and she and her daughter have a secure financial future. J.K. Rowling is now a billionaire and living her dream.

• **Overcome fear of failure.**
The fear of failure can be paralyzing. If you don't achieve your goal, you may think less of yourself or fear others might.

Negative outcomes do not define who you are. They are simply data points on the results of a particular course of action. Just by attempting something, you are learning things that can be leveraged into a new approach to achieving your goal. Many people think in extremes—all or nothing—and do not realize that they are getting value out of just trying to attain a goal. The fact that you are attempting your goal separates you from the great mass of people who don't even try. Their perception is that if they don't try at all, then they can't lose. In reality, by not trying they are losing out on living their dreams.

"You may be disappointed if you fail, but you are doomed if you don't try."
— Beverly Sills

• **Overcome fear of success.**
The two major reasons people fear success are the changes that may occur in their lives and the fear associated with a personal sense of power.

Success can bring about many changes in someone's life. Increased financial resources can lead to a new home, a different lifestyle, and new friends. If your goal does bring you great financial wealth, remember that you have the choice in how to manage that success. There is no reason your success has to separate you from the things you value most, whether they are the house you currently live in or the friends you love and cherish.

Warren Buffett, the famous multibillionaire, has chosen to live in the same house he bought three decades ago for $31,500.

Increased wealth may require an adjustment for you and your friends. However, the essence of who you are hasn't changed; you just have more resources. The qualities that attracted you to each other and that have sustained your friend-ships over the years remain the same. You will still have the same sense of humor, the same supportive qualities, the same degree of thoughtfulness and compassion. While you may now be able to afford lavish vacations or houses or accoutrements, you are basically the same person.

The other fear has to do with a greater awareness of your personal power. By achieving your goal, you have created a new level of success. The realization of that can make you feel uncomfortable. It may be easier to think that your life is being shaped solely by external factors and therefore you feel less responsible for your current circumstances. Once you realize that you have the power to create your own destiny you may not feel qualified for the job. Or you may feel that people are expecting more from you now. The truth is that you have always been in control of your life; however, you may not have been aware of it. Now that you are aware of your degree of control, there are no limits to what you can accomplish.

• Cope with the judgments of others.
People will definitely have opinions about what you are doing. There's no escaping that. Whether it's starting your own company or changing careers, some people may be supportive and some may not. You may be concerned about what people might think about your goal, your ability to achieve it, what it implies about you, how you will be impacted when you do achieve it, and other issues.

Feedback contrary to your goal can come from well-intentioned people who are looking out for your best interests. Their concern may be that you will be disappointed if you do not reach your goal. Or they may not think your goal is worth achieving. If they have a legitimate concern, take them through your thought process—why the goal is important and how you will attain it. The more information they have about your plan, the better they will be able to understand and support you.

There are many reasons people provide negative feedback. People may feel threat-ened by your potential success. Some people suffer from a great deal of insecurity and may not feel comfortable with another surpassing their level of success. While it may be difficult in the beginning, people do adjust to situations and generally come around. This is certainly the case with true friends.

One thing to remember is that people are generally resistant to change in themselves and others. When you announce your goal, it will signal that change is coming and it might make people feel uncomfortable. Let them know that your goal is consistent with your values and that you have an appropriate plan of action to achieve it. They may not see your goal as being right for you but only you can make that call.

• Know you are worthy.
People with high levels of self-esteem understand that mistakes are part of human nature. Their healthy self-image enables them to accept their shortcomings as being human and they continue believing they deserve good things.

Approach your goal today with the belief that you are worthy. Remember, mistakes are part of human nature and we all make them. Even if you have done things in the past that you believe are wrong, there's no benefit to classifying yourself as unworthy. If there is something about your character that you want to change, by all means do so. However, start pursuing your goal today, knowing that you deserve good things.

Conquering Procrastination

Procrastination can be effectively managed one decision at a time. It's the decision to do things when scheduled instead of at sometime in the future. When you scheduled your activities for your goal, you believed it was worthy of your time. Keeping that commitment is a conscious decision that will help you remain true to yourself.

There are obvious benefits to procrastination, which is why so many of us do it. If we put something off, then we can find something more fun to do, can forget about the project for a while, avoid doing the work, and avoid the prospect of failure. Whatever the reasons, understanding why you procrastinate is an important step to changing.

• Overcome lack of desire.
Some projects will be put off because, quite frankly, you just don't want to do them. You may have told yourself over and over again that this is something you should be working on, even though you don't want to do it. Ask yourself why you don't want to do it. Specifically, what are the advantages and disadvantages of starting the project? By evaluating your reasons, you may discover that this project is not right for you. Maybe this is something that you really don't need to do. If this is the case, and it is not a requirement of your job, now you can take it off your list. On the other hand, you may decide the project is right for you and choose to continue. Keep your reasons for wanting to continue at the front of your mind. This will help you keep moving forward.

Sometimes a certain phase of the project is so unmotivating that you will need to incorporate a reward for yourself for finishing that step. Decide beforehand what that reward will be. It can be very effective to link your efforts with a reward, especially when you are doing something you don't want to.

• Deal with hard projects.

Many people procrastinate on a project because the project is difficult. We can all relate to how frustrating it is when we are investing time, but not seeing the expected results. If something does not come easily, many times it's easier just to give up. Many people who accomplish their goals go in with the attitude that some phases may be difficult and they accept that. They are willing to dedicate more time and energy in order to get the results they want. Consequently, when they hit a wall, they are not surprised or discouraged because this is what they expected when they took on a difficult goal. If your project is particularly difficult, understand that it can be accomplished, but it may require more time and energy than you originally planned.

Sometimes we make a project more difficult than it needs to be by placing unreasonably high expectations on ourselves. You may have heard the expression, "Perfect is the enemy of good." Many of us procrastinate because when we approach a project, we set our standards too high. The pressure we put upon ourselves can lead to immobilizing stress and the result is that we do nothing. For some people, striving for excellence works. For others, it may be the reason things are not getting worked on. By balancing your high expectations with the realities of what is required, you will keep moving forward.

If your project seems daunting, one way to make it easier is to break it into its smallest parts and focus on one part at a time. You can also break it down into shorter work sessions. Working on a project for shorter periods of time can make it seem more doable and help keep you on track.

Importantly, when you work toward the completion of a project that is difficult, give yourself credit for making the effort.

• Don't wait for the right mood.

Many people wait until they are in the mood to work on their goal. They wait for the desire to do it. They erroneously believe that only by being in the mood will they be able to make headway. The reality is that progress can be made regardless of your mood. Even if some of your efforts might need to be reworked later, it is still more efficient to modify something you have already created than to start from scratch. Whatever action you take moves you closer to your goal.

The fact that you're not in the mood when you start can change during the activity. For example, you may not feel like going to the gym, but once you start working out you feel better. Working towards your goal, whether or not you are in the mood, is an achievement in itself.

"Eighty percent of success is just showing up."

—Woody Allen

• Overcome fatigue.

There may be times when your energy is sapped and you believe that you cannot work on your goal. This is experienced by many people, even high achievers. People who consistently achieve their goals do so partly by pushing through their low energy barriers. They find ways to re-energize themselves. From a physical standpoint, your body may need nourishment or stimulation—standing up, moving around, and stretching are all ways to signal your brain that you are ready.

Quite often, being tired is more a state of mind than a reality. For example, you are sitting at your desk feeling tired when your boss calls. He tells you that he needs a report in an hour. This report is going to take a lot more energy that you think you have. It's unlikely that you would tell your boss that you are too tired. Instead, you draw upon your energy reserves and complete the project. You muster the energy to do it, energy you didn't think you had.

The next time you are feeling too tired to work on your goal, remember you are the driver in this situation and can call upon your body to deliver what you need in order to advance your goal.

• Overcome distractions.

Approach the time you have set aside for your goal as if you were taking an important test. All your energies and focus are on a single topic. It's important for you to do well and you set yourself up for success. You approach each of these work sessions with one objective: At the end of the session, you have completed what you set out to do and feel good about your efforts.

It's easy to be interrupted at the office. To counteract this, let people know you will not be available during certain times or find a workplace that affords you the greatest likelihood of not being interrupted, like a private office or conference room.

• Continue to endeavor when under the weather.

Most of the time when you are not feeling well it will probably be the result of something minor. We have all encountered those days when we are not feeling up to par. Make it a point, even if you are not feeling your best, to try to make some progress toward your goal. Even if it's not an optimum effort, you are still making progress. Just as you may push yourself to go to work on a day when you're not feeling your best, use that same level of commitment to work toward your goal.

"Never put off to tomorrow what you can do today."

—Thomas Jefferson

Moving Past Frustrations

Successful people expect to face challenges, hurdles, and frustrations along the way; but they are not deterred by them. They put strategies in place for dealing with frustrations so that they can keep moving forward.

• Overcome plateaus.

With few exceptions, you should be able to spot a plateau within its first week. It will be the week that you are not seeing results even though your approach has remained the same. To effectively deal with this, you need to change something.

Evaluate all the components of your plan and identify a number of things you can start doing differently. For example, your goal may be to become a great motivational speaker. Even though you have been practicing every week, you haven't improved during the last few speeches. You identify things you can start changing: speaking more frequently, learning new speech techniques, and working with a personal coach. You decide to focus on just one of those things—to speak more often—and start seeing progress again. You have now overcome this plateau and know that if you should hit another, there are at least two additional options (new techniques and personal coach) for you to try.

Plateaus are a great opportunity to re-energize yourself by doing some things differently or trying new things.

• Handle unexpected events.

There are many things we just can't anticipate. Some people refer to this as "Murphy's Law"—what can go wrong will go wrong. Just when you were making real progress towards your goal, something unexpected intervenes and causes a setback.

For example, your marketing budget just got cut by $500,000. This means you will not have funds for a program to promote your new product. This program was key to achieving the product's annual sales goal. You may feel discouraged because your hard work will not be rewarded. Your bonus is tied to sales and it just became harder to reach your goal with a smaller budget.

Some people will lose enthusiasm for the product launch and miss opportunities to promote their product in other ways. They'll settle for the reduced sales and a reduced bonus. Others will roll up their sleeves and become more creative with a smaller budget. People in the latter group could end up with a decent bonus and recognition from senior management because they launched a successful product with fewer financial resources.

Your attitude of how you approach setbacks is key to achieving your goal.

• Deal with discouragement.

You may find yourself feeling discouraged at some point along the way and may even feel a sense of hopelessness about reaching your goal. Remember that although the negative thoughts may seem very real, most of them may be distorted and unrealistic.

One of the interesting things about moods—and discouragement is a mood—is that they are many times created by things we tell ourselves which simply are not true. These thoughts, which often have no basis in reality, can adversely affect your ability to actively pursue your goal. Discouragement can take many forms. Examples are: overgeneralization (where you take a single event and believe it is a pattern); discounting the positive (where you don't give yourself the proper credit); and personalization (where you hold yourself personally responsible for something that is not entirely under your control).

If you feel yourself becoming discouraged, examine your negative thoughts to see if they are based in truth. They may seem true, especially if you have repeated these negative thoughts often, but in all likelihood they are not. It is hard to be upbeat 100 percent of the time, but recognize that discouragement can be temporary and does not have to derail the pursuit of your goal.

Regaining Motivation

At the start of your goal, you are full of enthusiasm and energy. At the first sign of progress, you may be even more enthusiastic. At some point, however, your enthusiasm may wane. Loss of motivation happens at different points along the way for different people. For many people, the halfway mark is when they feel less motivation. For others, it may be toward the end. Regardless of when these feelings may occur, there are ways to rekindle your motivation so you can re-energize and move forward.

• **Keep in mind that your efforts are still worthwhile.**
Sometimes we lose focus on the bigger picture when we get too mired in the details. Even though you have made progress, your project may not be as fulfilling or seem worth the effort as you originally thought. This is common and what often helps reignite the fire is to get back in the mindset you had when you began. If your goal is something that you have been thinking about for a long time, there is a reason for that. Focus on that reason. Not every phase of your project will be equally fulfilling. However, reaching an important goal will make the effort feel worthwhile.

• **Stay excited.**
The excitement that you felt in the beginning can diminish and your course of actions can start to feel monotonous. This does not mean the goal is no longer valid. Astronauts, whose goal it has been to fly in space, sometimes get bored with the monotony of the preparation.

In the course of pursuing your goal, you may reach a point where you need to alter the routine. It might mean doing things in a different order, at a different time, in a different place, or doing something new. If you reach this point, look at the steps needed to accomplish your goal and re-evaluate them. Maybe there is a particular step that can be substituted for one you find more energizing. As long as any new approach moves you toward your goal, you can be flexible.

* * *

Hopefully, this chapter has helped you identify the areas where you are likely to stumble and has given you a new perspective on how to keep moving forward. Below is a list summarizing the thoughts that will help you maintain momentum. Photocopy or cut out the following list and put it somewhere handy. Whenever you find yourself not wanting to take the next scheduled action toward your goal, refer to this list and use it to keep yourself on track.

Maintain Momentum List

Building Self-Esteem
Believe you can do it. Knowing what didn't work in the past can serve you today. Use that knowledge and the persistence you demonstrate in other areas in your life to move toward your goal.

Release guilt. If you believe you should be doing, thinking, or feeling something else, remember the J.K. Rowling story. By investing in yourself you can enrich the lives of others.

Overcome fear of failure. Negative outcomes do not define who you are. They are simply information. Even in trying, there is a level of success because you are learning.

Overcome fear of success. Success may bring about changes; however, there is no reason those changes must separate you from the things and people you value most.

Cope with the judgments of others. People are resistant to change and may feel uncomfortable with your goal. Listen to their feedback and take them through your thought process. Let them know why this goal is important to you and how you will achieve it.

Know you are worthy. High achievers view their mistakes as part of being human, and they continue to believe they are worthy of good things. Apply this mindset to yourself and know that you are worthy.

Conquering Procrastination
Overcome lack of desire. Ask yourself why you may not want to do it. Maybe this is something that you really don't need to do. If you decide the project is right for you and choose to continue, keep your reasons for wanting to continue at the top of your mind.

Deal with hard projects. Break difficult projects into their smallest parts and focus on one part at a time. You can also break them down into shorter work sessions. High expectations can make a project seem harder than it is. Balancing your high expectations with the realities of what is required will help you keep moving forward.

Don't wait for the right mood. Sometimes action drives motivation and will get you into the mood. You don't have to "feel like it" to make progress—anything you do will move you closer to your goal. Eighty percent of success is just showing up. Show up today.

Overcome fatigue. Fatigue can be a state of mind. Successful people push through their low-energy barriers and so can you.

Overcome distractions. Find a workplace that affords you the greatest likelihood of success.

Continue to endeavor when under the weather. Even if you are not feeling 100 percent, try to make some progress toward your goal.

Moving Past Frustration

Overcome plateaus. Plateaus are opportunities to make changes in your routine—how and when you approach it. When you are not seeing results, even though your approach is the same, change something.

Handle unexpected events. Unexpected events do not have to derail you from your goal. Even if it feels like two steps forward and one step back, keep moving forward.

Deal with discouragement. Discouragement is just a mood created by things we tell ourselves, things which may not be true. Give yourself credit for how far you have come already.

Regain Motivation

Keep in mind that your efforts are still worthwhile. If you're getting mired down in the work, your goal may not feel worth the effort. Step back and look at the bigger picture. Think about how you will feel when you reach your goal. This will often put the work into perspective.

Stay excited. If things start to feel monotonous, you may need to alter your routine. Do things in a different order, at a different time, in a different place, or do something new.

* * *

Action Items   **Check When Done**

Photocopy or cut out the "Maintain
Momentum" list and put it someplace handy.

CHAPTER FIVE
How Others Reached the Top

One of the best ways we learn how to succeed ourselves is by understanding and relating to how other people were able to succeed. You may believe that successful people have some special talent that you do not have and that, in itself, explains how they were able to achieve their goals. Talent plays a part in success, but it is frequently not the main factor. It is an ability to overcome the obstacles along the way that makes all the difference between success and failure.

As a way to demonstrate just how successful people have overcome their obstacles, we have highlighted the individual stories of six well-known and extremely successful people in a wide diversity of industries.

Perhaps you will see yourself in one of these stories and use it as a source of inspiration for reaching your own goal. What you will notice is that no one is immune from setbacks and everyone faces challenges. What distinguishes the winners is that they figure out a way to reach their goals while dealing with the issues that are part of everyday living: fear of failure, too little time to work on their goals, unreasonable bosses, and many others too numerous to list.

It is important to remember that these are all regular people, just like us. They do not claim to be geniuses, but they demonstrate on a regular basis the drive that some people with greater native intelligence do not exhibit. They also demonstrate the creativity to recognize when a different tact is required in order to reach their goal. Being flexible is another key ingredient to success. When one approach does not yield the right results, they eagerly try something new.

What these stories illustrate is the importance of focusing on what you want and how you are going to get from the beginning of your goal to the end. Persistence is a key element to success. Do you remember playing tag as a child? If you were "It" and decided to set your sights on one person and doggedly set about chasing that person, never being deterred, eventually that person would find it easier to give up and let you tag him or her. Goals are the same way, in that they will surrender to the persistent person.

Anderson Cooper: A Passion for News

The story of Anderson Cooper, a well-known newsman, illustrates how thinking outside the box can catapult someone from the slow track to becoming a shining star. Taking an innovative approach to getting ahead can be a successful strategy for standing out from the crowd.

Anderson Cooper was ten-years old when his father died. It was an unexpected event that shook Anderson to his core. From this disaster he gained strength. He vowed to protect himself from further loss and decided he needed to earn his own money. "Even though my mother [Gloria Vanderbilt] was wealthy, I didn't want to rely on someone else." As life changing as this event was, it only grew more grim when, eleven years later, his older brother Carter committed suicide.

Anderson was in deep emotional pain. He thought he could learn how to survive this pain by being close to people who had experienced similar tragedies. "War seemed like my only option."

He decided to become a news correspondent and tried to get a job—any job—in a news station. After being turned down by a number of stations, he was finally offered an entry-level job as a fact checker at Channel One, a station broadcasting news to high schools. After months on the job, Anderson became bored and realized the only way he was going to get to report on the front lines was to take charge of his own future. He quit the station, borrowed a friend's video camera and, armed with a fake press pass, left for Thailand. He shot footage at the Thai-Burmese border of the Burmese refugees who were planning a government coup. Anderson's gamble paid off when he was able to sell the video to Channel One. Eighteen months later, his reporting career was launched when Channel One, where he had recently been a junior fact checker, now hired him as a correspondent.

After two years of compelling coverage in political hot spots like Bosnia, Croatia, and Rwanda, Anderson got an offer to join ABC News words as a correspondent, which just three years earlier had turned him down for an entry-level job. His initiative was paying off in a big way.

In December 2001, after the 9/11 attacks, Anderson accepted a position on CNN's program "American Morning." In March 2003, after the start of the war in Iraq, Anderson moved to prime time, hosting his own program, "Anderson Cooper 360."

While Anderson had reached a certain level of success, first in broadcasting and then anchoring, he really made his mark during his compelling coverage of Hurricane Katrina in 2005.

Because of the weather conditions, there was no teleprompter, no script to support his on-camera reporting: "I had to be quick on my feet, ready for anything." Anderson's interview with Louisiana State Senator Landrieu received national attention because of his emotionally charged questions. While Senator Landrieu went on and on thanking President Bush and senior ranking senators, Anderson grew impatient: "Excuse me Senator, sorry for interrupting. For the last four days I've been seeing dead bodies in the streets. And to listen to politicians thanking each other and complimenting each other.... There's a woman's body that's been on the street for forty-eight hours and there's not enough facilities to take her up. Do you get the anger that is out here?"

It was that kind of impassioned reporting that put Anderson on the map. Whether he was on the front lines of a war zone or a natural disaster, Anderson got emotionally involved in the stories he was covering and would occasionally get choked up during a broadcast. This ability to freely show his emotions while reporting the facts became a trademark of Anderson and clearly differentiated him from his broadcasting colleagues.

Broadcasting & Cable magazine wrote: "In its aftermath, Hurricane Katrina served to usher in a new breed of emo-journalism, skyrocketing CNN's Anderson Cooper to superstardom as CNN's golden boy and a darling of the media circles because of his impassioned coverage of the storm."

Anderson Cooper's success can be traced back to his unconventional approach and to trusting his instincts. He knew the shortest route to becoming a news correspondent was to get out there, do the job first, and then get hired. He trusted his instincts and it worked. The same could be said for his reporting style. He asked the questions his viewers wanted answered and wasn't afraid to show his emotions.

"I think you have to be yourself, and you have to be real and you have to admit what you don't know."

—Anderson Cooper

* * *

Like Anderson Cooper, you may be feeling boxed-in and unable to get to the next level. Is there an innovative approach you can take that would break the logjam? Your approach does not have to be as radical as the Cooper example. It could simply be a more original way of getting a job done.

Danielle Steele: Turning the Page to Best-Sellerdom

You would be hard pressed to find someone who has not heard of Danielle Steele. What her legions of readers may not know is just how hard she had to work to attain her present fame. More importantly, she continues to be a prolific writer after achieving wealth and fame.

Born on August 14, 1947, in New York City, Danielle described her childhood as "...disastrous. A lonely, heartbreaking, no-one-wanted-me kind of growing up." After her parents divorced, she was raised by her father, who for the most part was emotionally unavailable. Danielle felt terribly lonely and she escaped by reading. Her favorite author was Sidonie-Gabrielle Colette, a female writer whose novels were about love and betrayal. Out of this childhood of loneliness and despair, the seeds of a prolific author began to germinate.

In 1968, at the age of twenty, she started working at a public relations agency in New York. During a sales call she met John Mack Carter, the publisher at *Ladies' Home Journal*. He was impressed with Danielle and hired the agency. Danielle did some writing at the public relations firm and John Mack Carter liked her work. He encouraged her to write a book. With a story idea in mind, Danielle spent the entire summer of 1971 holed up working on her first manuscript, *Going Home*. This intensive approach to writing, eighteen hours a day with no breaks, would characterize her style and continue throughout her career, allowing her to write multiple books per year. To her delight, *Going Home* was published in 1973.

Between 1972 and 1973, Danielle wrote her next four books and a screenplay. Her agent couldn't find a publisher for any of the manuscripts. In fact, one work received twenty-seven rejection slips. "Before I could get discouraged, I had already written my next book," she recalls. This tenacious, not-to-be-denied approach provided little time for Danielle to worry about rejection. She was in the process of developing and honing her writing style, one which would captivate a country—and then a worldwide audience.

Her writing regimen was to block out several days, allowing nothing to interrupt: "If you let anything infringe on your time, it will, and you won't get the writing done." This work ethic served her well, and her next book, *Passion's Promise*, was published in 1977. Later that year, Danielle received a call that would drastically change her life. It was Universal Studios calling to ask Danielle to take on a project. They wanted her to adapt a screenplay, *The Promise*, written by Gary White, into a novel. Universal Studios needed a romance novelist to write the book and needed it done quickly, before the movie's release. The studio was banking on this film being a huge success and it had committed the unheard of sum of $500,000 to promote the book. Danielle went to work, churning out the pages and turned in the completed manuscript, which was published in 1978. The book was a huge success and became a bestseller with two million copies in print. This put Danielle on the map. Unfortunately for the movie studio, the film did not do well. One notable difference between the script and the novel was that Danielle altered the conclusion so that readers were left with a happy ending. The happy ending gave readers what they craved, and this would become her trademark.

Danielle continued to crank out one bestseller after another in rapid succession. While her books were incredibly successful they were not taken seriously by the literary scene and she often received criticism for her writing style and unrealistic plots. She never received the critical acceptance she thought she deserved: "Negative reviews are like baking a cake with all the best ingredients and having someone sit on it." While professional reviewers were critical, Danielle's readers were very loyal and fan clubs started cropping up across the country. She had struck a powerful chord with romance readers, who devoured her books. This success changed the genre in the industry as publishers became comfortable extending romance novels to hardcover.

In 1983, Danielle hired a new agent to take her career to the next level—films. It had been her dream to see her novels appear on the big screen. Her 1983 book, *Now and Forever*, became a made-for-TV movie; however, it didn't do well. Importantly, that momentary failure did not deter Danielle from continuing to pursue her dream. Her earlier novel, *Crossings*, was optioned and became a success as an ABC miniseries. Over twenty films would follow.

Today, Danielle Steele is one of the most prolific and best-selling authors in the United States. She has sold more than 570 million copies of her novels, and she is listed in the *Guinness Book of World Records* for being on the *New York Times* bestseller list for over 381 consecutive weeks. The editors of the book were premature—the actual number of weeks ran to 390.

Danielle's formula for success was simple: Do what you love doing, find what works, and stick with it. Even in the face of setbacks, keep moving forward. From her childhood loneliness came the impetus for a bestselling author who continues today to set a daunting pace for productivity. Danielle's loyal fan base is a testament to her success.

"I try to give people hope. Even though life is bleak, there's hope out there."
—Danielle Steel

* * *

As you undertake your goal, ask yourself if you are consistently performing at a high level. Consistency is the key to getting what you want.

Richard Branson: The Sky's the Limit

Most people recognize the face of Richard Branson, but far fewer people know the story of how he achieved greatness. His story of dealing with risk is an excellent lesson for every entrepreneur-to-be. His unwillingness to accept the status quo with regard to his company helped propel him into the upper echelon of business leaders.

Born in England in 1950, Richard Branson was always a bit of a maverick. Early on in his life, he wanted to be a journalist. While attending Stowe, a public school in Buckinghamshire, he would spend his afternoons in the school library, writing a novel. After winning a contest for writing a short story, Richard was convinced he was on the right path.

Like most British schools, the rules at Stowe were fairly strict. One rule in particular rankled Richard, as it required every student to watch the school team when they were playing against other teams in matches. For Richard, this meant less time to further his writing ambitions. He complained to the headmaster, who suggested Richard write his views in the school newspaper.

Displaying the ingenuity that would later launch a conglomerate, Richard decided instead to start his own publication where he would be free to espouse all his revolutionary ideas. The magazine was called *Student* and before long it became very popular. Spending most of his free time managing the paper, he became aware of the issues that were important to the students and how he could bring change to those things. One of the things Richard understood about students was that they would forgo meals in order to save money to buy records. He also realized there were no stores selling discounted records and decided to create a business focused on this void. The name "Virgin" was proposed by a partner who correctly assessed that they were "Virgins in business."

Virgin was a mail-order business at first and did quite well. However, in 1971, the company was almost ruined by a postal strike. Richard knew this strike would essentially cripple the business. Displaying the flexibility that came to characterize his business philosophy, within a week he used all the company's funds to open a record store. He made sure the store would cater to students, giving them an atmosphere where they would feel comfortable spending as much time as they wanted. Virgin customers were offered headphones to sample the music, beanbag chairs to relax in, and free coffee. Richard hoped that the more time his customers spent in the store, the more records they might buy.

By Christmas of 1972, Virgin had fourteen record shops.

As a retailer, Richard wasn't affected by the success or failure of an individual band. That was the good news. The bad news, however, was that his profits were limited to a small retail margin. Never one to settle for the status quo, Richard decided to grow the business by leveraging what he already knew about records to make more money.

He knew that record companies had formal rules for recording artists—strict appointment times, requirements to bring their own equipment, and stringent timetables as to when they needed to leave the studios. Richard saw an opportunity to offer a freer-flowing environment in which bands could record music. By renting out studio space he could earn higher profits. Seizing on the opportunity, he bought a house in the country and set up a recording studio with state-of-the-art equipment. Bands began to rent the space and Richard once again had a thriving business.

He was a master at leveraging one business in order to create another, and a year later Richard decided to start a record company. During the past year, one musician, Mike Oldfield, had been using the studio on a regular basis. Fortunately for Richard, he found out that Mike had not been signed by any record company. In 1972, Richard signed Mike Oldfield as Virgin's first recording artist. To their delight and good fortune, Mike Oldfield turned out to be a big success.

The company continued to sign new bands; however, Mike Oldfield was the only successful artist. It was 1976 and all the other bands were losing money.

Virgin was in financial trouble. It was a turning point for Richard and his partners. The company could cut all the other bands and make a comfortable living riding on Mike Oldfield's success, or use the last bit of cash they had to sign a breakout artist: "If we chose the first option, we could get by: We would be running a tiny company, but we could survive making a living without any risks attached. If we chose the second, Virgin could be bust within a few months, but at least we would have one last chance to break out."

Once again displaying his penchant for taking a calculated risk, Richard decided to "go for it," eventually signing The Sex Pistols, Phil Collins, The Human League and Boy George. Virgin became a huge success and the money flowed. Acknowledging the wisdom of establishing multiple sources of income, Richard used the money to create other Virgin companies, "So that all of our eggs wouldn't be in one basket."

Ever the entrepreneur, Richard was soon looking for another new idea, one that would excite him. When that idea arrived, it came from left field. A lawyer was looking for investors to finance a new airline offering service from New York to Gatwick (London). He sent Richard a proposal. Richard's mind began to formulate a plan that would minimize the risks—if they could lease a plane for a year and then be able to return it if the business failed, that would limit the amount of losses. In 1984, the only airline offering cheap flights across the Atlantic was People Express. Richard phoned People Express and continually received a busy signal. This made him believe that either they were poorly managed or there was so much demand they couldn't handle the calls. Either way, there was room for new competition. In 1984, Virgin Atlantic made its debut.

In the years that followed, Richard continued to add companies under the Virgin umbrella. He applied the same strategy to make all of them successful. He invested in areas that he was passionate about. He capitalized on what was missing in the marketplace and grew his competitive advantage. Above all, he was a genius at managing risks along the way. He had an uncanny ability to take calculated risks. Whether those risks were staying small versus scaling, expanding from one revenue stream to multiple streams, or entering new industries, Branson managed risks effectively. Today, Virgin Group has created more than 200 companies in twenty-nine countries and has 50,000 employees. Revenues in 2006 were approximately $20 billion.

"My interest in life comes from setting huge, apparently unachievable challenges and trying to rise above them."

—Richard Branson

* * *

Most goals involve taking risks. This is inherent in going outside of your comfort zone. Take calculated risks, and recognize that you can't steal second base with your foot on first.

Ellen DeGeneres: Programmed for Success

Ellen DeGeneres' story is one of finding her true calling—comedy—and then working her way up the ranks in the extremely competitive entertainment world. She dealt with the inevitable struggles to get to the top and then overcame a major disappointment to reach even greater heights.

The comedienne was born on January 26, 1958, in Metairie, Louisiana, the daughter of two devoutly religious Christian Scientists. Her parents split up when she was thirteen and shortly after that, she and her mother moved to New Orleans.

Her mother was depressed after the divorce, and in an effort to lift her mother's spirits, Ellen tried comedy and discovered she had a talent for being funny. "The divorce made me realize how important humor was," Ellen now says. "As a thirteen-year-old kid, to realize that you can manipulate somebody and make them happy is a really powerful thing." She had an epiphany of sorts: "To know that I could make my mom feel good started pushing me toward comedy; that's when I started working on it."

Following high school graduation in 1976, DeGeneres worked a variety of low-paying jobs, while she tried to figure out what she wanted to do with her life. She was not thinking about comedy as a career at this point.

Ellen spent a semester at the University of New Orleans. She was a communications student, but could not get interested in any of the coursework: "I hated school, but I started college because everyone else was going. I just remember sitting in there and they were talking about the history of the Greek theater or something and thinking, 'This is not what I want to know.'"

Dropping out of college, her future was anything but clear. She took a succession of low-paying jobs while trying to find something that would spark her interest as a possible career. Ellen would hold various jobs for short periods of time, depending on its ability to hold her attention—but never for very long. She worked at a car wash, baby sat, wrapped packages in a department store, worked as an accountant for a wig store, became a clothing salesperson at a local chain store, was a hostess and bartender at a restaurant, worked briefly (four hours) as a landscaper and even was a vacuum cleaner salesperson.

At her various jobs, Ellen would display her sense of humor, and coworkers encouraged her to try her hand at stand-up comedy. Ellen's first formal effort was at a luncheon benefit during which she used virtually no material—just sat and ate her lunch in front of the audience, interspersing a few sentences in between bites of a hamburger, while they waited for her to tell jokes. To her amazement, the "bit" worked. This led to her first gig at a coffeehouse and then more stand-up engagements at various universities in Louisiana, including Tulane and Loyola.

In 1982, she entered Showtime's "Funniest Person in America" contest and won. Shortly thereafter, she moved to San Francisco, one of the centers for stand-up comedy. Her signature routine was a telephone call to God that had been inspired by a close friend's accidental death in New Orleans. She used the piece during her debut on Johnny Carson's "Tonight Show" in 1986. Impressed with Ellen's talent, Carson invited her to sit upon his couch, an honor that he bestowed upon only the most gifted comics. She was the first female comic to be so honored by him.

Afterward, her career exploded with a cross-country tour and a few specials on cable television. Then came the "Ellen" show on ABC, which was based largely on DeGeneres' comedy. It was very popular and she garnered two Emmy nominations for her role.

In 1997, DeGeneres created a buzz with hints that her character on the show was gay and would come out of the closet later that season. It was a bold move, one made even more titillating to audiences by rumors that DeGeneres herself was gay. Ellen, the character, came out of the closet at the end of April 1997. Not surprisingly, the episode generated high ratings and considerable controversy, for it was the first time an openly gay character starred on a television show. At the same time, DeGeneres announced that she, too, was gay. The show centered on gay themes from that point.

To her shock and disappointment, the show was cancelled in 1998 due to low ratings. Her career up until then had been a steady climb upward, with each year bringing greater success. However, after climbing to the top of the mountain in television, she suddenly plummeted to the bottom.

Though extremely disappointed, DeGeneres continued to perform. In 1998, she costarred as a detective in the feature comedy "Goodbye Lover." She did not let her disappointment keep her from continuing to work on her craft.

Ellen had the usual self-doubts that plague most people. However, she had a positive attitude about whatever her perceived shortcomings might be: "People say *'You're no good. You're not pretty enough. You're not small enough.'* But you gotta just keep walking. You got to keep up and say *'I can make it.'*" It was this spirit of persistence that enabled Ellen to keep moving forward. Success, in a new form, was just around the corner.

In 2003, Ellen was approached about developing her own talk show. Watching the other talk shows hosts, she knew that the only way to be successful was to be herself on camera, just as Johnny Carson, Jay Leno, and David Letterman were. One of the epiphanies that Ellen had was that going through the ups and downs of her career had made her appreciate her current successes all the more.

Ellen DeGeneres' success continues as her talk show maintains its strong ratings. She is a great example of the importance of a positive attitude and the perseverance to keep going in the face of setbacks.

"I'm so grateful for every step of the way because it makes me appreciate this time even more. I feel like the success is even sweeter."

—Ellen DeGeneres

* * *

Most likely, achieving your goal will involve overcoming hurdles and disappointments. The important thing to remember is to keep moving forward. No matter what they are, these obstacles will yield to your efforts.

James Dyson: Inventing in a Vacuum

Here is the story of an inventor who simply was too determined to take "No" for an answer. His belief in the effectiveness of his product enabled him to relentlessly pursue his dream.

James Dyson was born in 1947, in the town of Norfolk, England. His father was a schoolteacher and the family lived in a huge Victorian house.

In 1956, at age nine, James' father died of cancer. The loss of his father meant that James did not have that important same-sex parent resource to turn to when he was experiencing troubles as a boy. The fact that he spent his youth trying to figure things out for himself made him more self-reliant and more of a fighter.

An early lesson for James was seeing his father about to change careers, from teaching to broadcasting—and then dying just before he was about to start his new career with the BBC: "Seeing him thwarted by death in that way, having done something else for so long, made me determined that that should never happen to me: I would not be dragged into something I didn't want to do."

His interest in mechanical things started when he would visit for a couple of weeks each summer with his friend, Michael Brown. Michael's father was mechanically inclined and would show the boys how to make gas engines and small steam engines in his workshop. James enjoyed these times, but it did not immediately translate into a career aspiration.

He thought his true calling might be as an artist and he enrolled in art school. This was to be an important time for James, as he learned to think in three dimensions.

He was an early admirer of the architecture of Buckminster Fuller, the creator of the geodesic dome, which was patented in 1954 and reproduced several hundred thousand times since then. James admired the fact that Fuller was not taken seriously in his early years: "Buckminster Fuller knew well that the only way to make a genuine breakthrough was to pursue a vision with single-minded determination in the face of criticism. If you try to change things, then you upset the establishment, which is why invention and vilification have always gone hand in hand."

By 1969, James had explored a number of potential career options: painting, designing furniture, interior design, and engineering. One of his first successes was an air-lubricated polyurethane landing craft. He sold 250 of them and it was a financial success.

After an unsuccessful attempt at marketing a Ballbarrow (a version of the wheelbarrow), James Dyson launched the product that would become synonymous with his name: the Dyson Vacuum Cleaner. Although vacuum cleaners were introduced commercially in 1908 by W. H. Hoover, little innovation had taken place in the category for about seventy years. While using a vacuum cleaner at home in 1978, James noticed that the cleaner lost suction when the bag had only a fine coating of dust on it. This surprised him, as he expected that the bag would have to be full or nearly so in order to cause the suction power to decline dramatically. James was annoyed because he had spent a lot of money on what was purported to be the most powerful vacuum cleaner—a Hoover—ever produced. No matter what the latest iteration was, the vacuum cleaner was inherently just as bad as its predecessor.

Dyson opined: "As far as the vacuum revolution was concerned, revolution was over." Had it not been for James Dyson, this trend of non-innovation might well have continued indefinitely.

As an outgrowth of solving a problem at the plant that was producing the Ballbarrow, Dyson latched on to the concept of the cyclone, a cone that would spin dust out of the air by centrifugal force. He created a model using his old Hoover vacuum as a starting point. Using cardboard, he revamped the insides of the cleaner. He began vacuuming his house, not quite knowing what to expect. To his amazement and delight, the suction of the vacuum remained at a high level and there was no bag to clog. He was, as he put it, "the only man in the world with a bagless vacuum cleaner."

The product development process was a laborious one, as he made cyclones day after day, working all day on making new versions of the cyclone: acrylic cyclones, rolled-brass cyclones, machined aluminum cyclones.

Most people would have given up, but he doggedly kept up this exhausting practice of trial and error for three years, while creating 5,127 different models trying to perfect the product. During this time, he used up the money he had borrowed and his home mortgage grew steadily bigger. Acknowledging his need to finally make some money from his invention, he tried to license it to manufacturers. The benefit of licensing was that he would not have to be involved in management or problems on the production lines and the concerns that arise from having a large staff.

He approached a litany of potential customers—Hotpoint, Electrolux, Goblin, AEG, Electrostar, Alfatech, Shopvac, Black & Decker, Zanussi, and Hamilton Beach—all with the same negative result. He was incredulous and frustrated that no one was interested in his revolutionary vacuum cleaner. One cause for these turndowns was best expressed by the comment that Electrolux made, that they "made a lot of money selling bags and this product did not use bags."

A Japanese company, Apex, liked his concept and afforded him the resources to make the product better. This vacuum cleaner, known as the G-Force, was introduced in Japan in 1986 and the cost was roughly $3,000 per unit. Dyson believes it was the high cost of the product that made it successful in Japan. "Despite, or perhaps because of, its enormous price, it soon became *the* must-have domestic style-item for the fashionable man or woman about Tokyo."

Deciding to take the product to market in the United Kingdom in the early 1990s, James chose an advertising agency to help him rapidly gain awareness for the Dual Cyclone product, DC-01. His advertising agency came up with the theme line "Say Goodbye to the Bag."

By 1995, the Dyson DC-01 had become the best-selling vacuum cleaner in the UK. In that same year the follow up product, the Dyson Dual Cyclone DC-02, was introduced to market and quickly became the second fastest-selling vacuum cleaner. James Dyson was hitting his stride. In 2002, Dyson introduced his vacuum products to the United States and met with immediate success.

It had taken James Dyson fifteen years and more than 5,000 prototypes to launch his revolutionary vacuum cleaner. The essence of James Dyson is summed up in these words:

"The most I can hope for, that my own story, the non-secret of my success, will inspire other people to go out and make things…and keep hold of their dreams."
—James Dyson

* * *

Keep your goal in the forefront of your mind and don't take "No" for an answer.

Vera Wang: Down the Aisle and Up the Ladder

She is a household name today, but it wasn't always so. The story of Vera Wang reminds us that, despite initial success in our careers, it is nonetheless daunting to consider starting our own business. Hers is a story that reflects the personality behind the successful business woman.

Vera Wang is one of the world's foremost fashion designers, best known for her signature bridal gowns, which sell for upwards of $20,000. Celebrities such as Mariah Carey and Sharon Stone are among her clients. Nowadays, women are used to having a variety of choices when it comes to wedding gowns, but it wasn't always so. Before Vera Wang got into the wedding gown business, bridal gowns had been stuck in a design rut that included antique lace and poufs. Vera capitalized on the lack of current fashion and made her mark by modernizing the look of bridal gowns.

Vera Wang grew up in Manhattan in a privileged household and graduated from prestigious Sarah Lawrence College. After living in Paris and studying at the Sorbonne, she knew that her future lay in fashion: "I wanted something to do with fashion. I would have done anything. I would have swept floors. I would have licked envelopes. I just wanted to be part of it." Her passion was so strong and she dreamed one day of having her own line.

Her first job in the fashion industry began while she was still in college, working summers as a salesgirl at Yves Saint Laurent on Madison Avenue. Putting herself in that environment enabled her to meet an editor from *Vogue*, who encouraged her to call when she graduated. Vera did just that and was soon working at *Vogue*.

Vogue turned out to be a dream job. At age twenty-three, she was one of the youngest editors in the history of the magazine. She worked for *Vogue* for sixteen years and, although successful, she longed to be closer to the design part of the industry. She left *Vogue* to join Ralph Lauren as a design director. A few years later, at age forty, she was engaged to be married.

In a serendipitous turn of events, Vera was led to the bridal gown business by her frustration at trying to find her own wedding gown. She couldn't find a wedding dress that excited her. Frustrated, she designed her own gown and commissioned a dressmaker to tailor the wedding dress at a cost of $10,000. Believing that this was a problem that many brides-to-be experienced, a lightbulb went off in her head. This design challenge could be the vehicle for launching her line of fashion.

This was easier said than done. Vera's entire career, although successful, had been in the confines of the corporate world, where the risks were mitigated by teams of support staff and a corporate hierarchy. The thought of going out on her own was daunting. She was terrified that she would fail after all the years she had spent building her career. While working as a design director at Ralph Lauren, she knew the difficulty in manufacturing, shipping, and selling a line of clothing. She knew she had talent, but she also knew that running a successful business required other skills.

Rather than focusing on her fears, she pushed forward and pursued her dream. In 1990, she opened the first Vera Wang bridal boutique: "I remember signing a lease for the store thinking, this is my death warrant, because how am I going to pay this rent?"

The Vera Wang label quickly took off, with her wedding gowns selling for around $3,000. Profits, however, weren't as significant as she had hoped. Vera looked for ways to increase demand, and did so by focusing on providing exceptional service to the brides. Her company helped women select bridesmaids' dresses, jewelry, shoes, etc. This personal touch helped drive sales and, as Wang declared, "I'm creating an image, a brand, and a name."

After years of hard work, she did just that.

In 2006, her sales had grown to approximately $300 million dollars. Over the years, she has extended her line to include sportswear and evening gowns, and licenses her name for a myriad of other products such as eyewear, crystal, china, jewelry, linens, and more. She owns two boutiques in New York, along with stores in Athens, Shanghai, Singapore, Seoul, and Jakarta. In 2008, she launched a more affordable line called "Simply Vera," which is sold exclusively at Kohl's.

Vera Wang did many things right. She identified a niche in the marketplace, used her success in bridal gowns as a platform for other products, and, above all, didn't let fear stop her from pursuing her dream.

Her tenacity, vision, and courage have been an inspiration:

"Nothing replaces hard work."

—Vera Wang

Fear of failure can be paralyzing. Challenge the assumptions behind your fear. By shining the light on it (fear lives in the dark), you'll be able to assess whether these fears are warranted. Ask yourself, what is the worse case scenario? How likely is that to happen? Regardless, wouldn't it still be worth attempting?

* * *

Hopefully, these examples have demonstrated that even the most successful people face obstacles to reaching their goals. All of them showed the inner strength necessary to overcome the hurdles and continue on. The roadblocks were different for each individual, but their reaction to the roadblocks was virtually identical: find a way to overcome them.

As you begin the journey toward your goal, keep in mind that there will be obstacles for you to deal with, but you will find a way to overcome them and ultimately reach your goal. Every goal, no matter how daunting, will be attainable if you just keep working at it, doing the right things at the right time.

During the course of working toward your goal, you may find it beneficial to refer back to some of the material that has been presented in the first six chapters. If you need a dose of inspiration to keep you going when things are tough, be sure to re-read this chapter in order to remind yourself that even the most successful people in their respective fields had to deal with adversity in order to reach the top.

CHAPTER SIX
Believe

How you look at something has everything to do with its outcome. A positive attitude, one of confidence, optimism, and belief is the most important factor in your ability to achieve your goal. It is essential to your success.

Belief comes from knowing that all that you need in order to fulfill your dream is presently within you: the aptitude, the desire, the energy, and the will to draw upon those assets.

It takes two things to believe in yourself. The first is the acknowledgement that you have the resources to be successful. The second is the understanding that your past experiences will support you in your endeavor.

Your Current Position of Strength

Taking stock of your current assets will allow you to believe in your ability to be successful. These assets include your finances, your health, your friendships, your family, and your character. All these are resources that can support you in the pursuit of your goal.

Many times we focus on what is missing in our lives and don't take the time to appreciate all the good things that we have created. There are probably many things in your life that you are grateful for and many more you haven't even considered.

Famous American psychiatrist Abraham Maslow is best known for his "Hierarchy of Needs"—a pyramid representation of the various stages of a person's needs. At the lowest level is food and water. Once a person has satisfied this need they focus on the next, which is safety and security. Then comes being loved and belonging. The fourth level is the need for esteem—recognition and acceptance from other people, self-confidence, and competence. At the top level is self-actualization—the need humans have to make the most of their abilities and to strive to be their best.

You may not have realized how close you are to self-actualization. The fact that you are pursuing your goal indicates that you are close—if not at—the top of the pyramid.

Your Past Can Serve You

When it comes to evaluating your own past experiences you may incorrectly believe:

- Unfavorable results are what you can mostly expect from yourself.
- What you may have been told about your abilities being limited is true.

The path to success is often strewn with negative outcomes. It is when we internalize these outcomes that they become inhibiting. Thomas Edison is a clear example of someone who didn't allow his 10,000 failed experiments to affect him on a personal level. Those experiments, like your past experiences, can support you in learning what works. If you take the time to examine the specifics involved in each one of your negative outcomes, you can extract kernels of wisdom that you can utilize in the pursuit of your goal.

Take heart from these people who used their past unsuccessful experiences to serve them:

- R.H. Macy was unsuccessful seven times in retail before his store in New York became famous.
- Babe Ruth struck out 1,330 times, but also hit 714 home runs.
- Abraham Lincoln ran a country store, went broke, ran for the House and lost twice, ran for the Senate and lost twice, delivered a speech that became a classic but was despised by half the country. Despite all this, he became the most admired president in U.S. history.

All three of these individuals viewed their unsuccessful attempts as part of the process to reach their ultimate goal. Whether they were discouraged or not, they kept moving forward. As you consider your own personal history, recognize that your past negative outcomes aren't a predictor of similar outcomes in the future.

What Macy, Ruth, and Lincoln had was a strong belief in their ability to be successful. By incorporating a strong belief in yourself, you will create the platform for success.

If you lived in an environment where you were told that your abilities were limited, chances are you took this at face value. As a child, the opinions you received from such authority figures as parents and teachers carried extra weight because you believed they understood the world. Naturally, you believed what they told you. Like grooves on a record, those opinions became ingrained in your mind without your questioning their validity. Or maybe the authority figures in your life didn't expect much from you and over the course of your life you incorporated these lower expectations into your belief system.

As a mature person, you are now in a position to challenge these assumptions. If you were told that you were not good at something specific, trace that back to its origin. Evaluate whether or not it *was* or *is* true. Rather than aligning yourself with these negative opinions and defining yourself accordingly, picture yourself at the other end of the spectrum, where you are successful.

It's not the events that occur, but the way we interpret them, that shapes who we believe we are and who we believe we will become. It's not what happens to you but what you do with what happens to you that matters.

Believe in the Best Outcome

The bestselling classic, *The Power of Positive Thinking*, by Norman Vincent Peale, was written in 1952 and has sold over five million copies. It is as relevant today as it was more than fifty years ago.

In his book, Dr. Peale writes, "To learn to believe is of primary importance. It is the basic factor of succeeding in any undertaking. When you expect the best, you release a magnetic force in your mind which by law of attraction tends to bring the best to you. It is amazing how a sustained expectation of the best, sets in motion forces which cause the best to materialize."

Becoming a believer and expecting good things to happen will result in achieving whatever it is that you want. And whatever that thing is, you must want it wholeheartedly. Throw yourself into your goal and let your passion come through. There is no greater feeling of satisfaction than doing what you love.

> *"The thing always happens that you really believe in; and the belief in the thing makes it happen."*
>
> —Frank Lloyd Wright

Practice believing in success and hold that picture in your mind.

You Are Successful

There are many things you already do successfully. Whatever these things are, you approach them knowing with 100-percent certainty that you will achieve what you want. Approach your goal with this high level of certainty and what you set out to do will be accomplished. When you start on your action items, bring an attitude of success. This mental attitude will create the desired outcome. When you encounter an obstacle, approach it with the idea that you will overcome it without question. This thinking will penetrate your subconscious and all your energies will be focused on delivering optimum results.

The Story of Roger Bannister

One of the most famous achievements in the world of individual sports belongs to Roger Bannister, who was the first person to break track racing's four-minute mile barrier. He is an excellent example of how believing and expecting a certain outcome can lead to success.

In 1946, while studying medicine at Oxford University, Roger spent every moment he could training as a middle-distance runner. During that time it was widely believed that it was humanly impossible to run a mile in under four minutes. Roger believed it *was* possible and felt it was just another record that could be broken. After failing to medal in the 1952 Olympics, Roger was devastated, as he had been the medal hopeful for England. Because of this major disappointment, Roger considered giving up running altogether. However, because running was his dream, Roger pushed on and established an even more aggressive goal for himself: to be the first to break the four-minute mile.

With the help of two friends, Chris Brasher and Chris Chataway, both accomplished runners, Roger planned a strategy to accomplish his goal. Brasher and Chataway would alternate setting a record-breaking pace for Roger to follow. Since neither friend could maintain that pace throughout the race, they would take turns leading Roger.

It was in 1954 at Iffley Road in England that Roger Bannister took on the challenge. With spectators and photographers lining the track, Roger toed the starting line. When the race started, Chris Brasher took the lead and set the pace for the first half mile. Bannister was right behind him and Chataway was third. Then Chataway took the lead, with Roger in second place. Two hundred and fifty yards from the finish line, Roger Bannister sprinted past Chataway, crossed the finish line and collapsed into the crowd. The roar from the crowd followed the announcement of his historic time of 3:59.04, breaking the four-minute barrier by six tenths of a second! Roger Bannister had become the first person to run a mile in under four minutes.

By believing in the possibility of his goal and expecting to break the record, Roger had broken a psychological and physical barrier. Years later, Bannister became an accomplished neurologist. However, he will always be remembered as the man who ran the "miracle mile."

As You Begin the 30-DAY GOAL TRACK

You are about to embark on an exciting journey that will result in achieving the goal you are currently focused on. All your hard work will pay off and overcoming subsequent challenges in the future will become second nature.

This is an exciting time. You have identified your goal and mapped out a plan to achieve it. As you work toward your goal, we are there with you in the form of the

30-DAY GOAL TRACK. Think of this as the training wheels on your first bike. It is here to steady you, give you confidence, and keep you moving forward.

As you get in the habit of doing these exercises, you will find yourself consistently working on your goal. That consistency is the key to success. Even small efforts done consistently over time will eventually lead to your desired outcome.

Hindsight is always 20/20. If you knew, right now, that you would definitely achieve the goal you are about to undertake, you would approach it with confidence, with full energy—none would be dissipated in negative thoughts—and any obstacles would be tackled with authority. This is the mind-set we want you to have for the next thirty days. If you are able to do this, you will easily carry that attitude forward in the months that follow.

Because we know that this high level of confidence is the key to your success, the exercises were created with the assumption that you have already achieved your goal. *When someone starting out on a goal assumes they have already reached that goal, it reinforces that they can and will do it.*

Your goal, what you are about go after, is important. Achieving that goal is worth your time, energy, and commitment. Making it a priority is the right thing to do because reaching your goal is truly living your life to the fullest.

Let's get started!

"In the arena of life, the honors and rewards fall to those who show their good qualities in action."

—Aristotle

PHASE II

The 30-Day Goal Track

For the next thirty days you will have a daily assignment, either an exercise or a short reading, to help you stay motivated. The exercises are situational and assume the perspective that you have already reached your goal.

While doing each assignment, imagine that you have already achieved the goal you set out to do, because, as we have discussed, this will create a mind-set of success.

These exercises are hypothetical and their purpose is to reinforce how you will feel when you achieve your goal.

The 30-Day Goal Track has been created in a specific order for your benefit, so it will be important for you to do each day's assignment in succession. The key will be consistency and, in that regard, make it the utmost priority to do one assignment each day rather than accumulating several days of assignments for completion all at once.

As a reminder, you are trying to develop habits that will help you reach this goal and others in the future. The assignments will typically take five minutes each day and will not require preplanning.

Keys for Success with the 30-Day Goal Track:

- Do the assignments in the morning, if at all possible.
- If you fall behind, do not try to play catch-up. Simply start in on the next assignment, continuing the one-day-at-a-time approach.
- If your visuals and affirmations from Chapter Three are losing impact, change them to ones that are more meaningful to you.

- Some exercises require more thought than others. If you have trouble with any particular one, it's better to write something down than to skip it all together.

The journey toward achieving your goal is about to begin and you have everything you need in order to be successful.

DAY 1
The Finish Line

"The journey of a thousand miles starts with a single step."

—Lao-Tzu

You have achieved your goal and to your delight, your friends and family members are throwing a small celebration for you tonight.

During the course of the evening, someone asks you to describe to everyone the day you knew you would make it to the finish line.

Write down your response to this request.

_____

_____

_____

_____

_____

_____

_____

_____

GOAL!

Action Items   **Check When Done**

- Affirmations

- Visualizations—images

- Close your eyes for two minutes and
  experience the feelings of having
  achieved your goal

- Day 1's assignment

- Today's scheduled Action Items from
  your calendar

Countdown: 29 days until you are in the habit of working toward your goal.

DAY 2
Expanding Your Scope

—Quote for the day—

"All adventures, especially into new territory, are scary."

—Sally Ride

Your boss calls an urgent meeting with you and your peers. She tells everyone that she has to go out of town for an unexpected customer meeting and needs someone to take her place as a speaker in a seminar tomorrow night. All of you are capable of filling in. She asks for a volunteer and, to your surprise, you raise your hand. You are chosen and do a great job the following night.

Upon reflection, you realize that because you have accomplished your goal it is easier for you to take on new challenges.

Describe how this feels.

_____

_____

_____

_____

_____

Action Items	Check When Done
• Affirmations	☐
• Visualizations—images	☐
• Close your eyes for two minutes and experience the feelings of having achieved your goal	☐
• Day 2's assignment	☐
• Today's scheduled Action Items from your calendar	☐

Countdown: 28 days until you are in the habit of working toward your goal.

DAY 3
Mentoring Lindsey

Lindsey, at twenty-five-years old, is a likable young lady who works in your company. She is thinking about going to back to school and getting her MBA. She is very capable at work and there is no reason to believe she'll be any less capable in school. Still, she has doubts about her ability to achieve her goal of getting a master's degree.

Help Lindsey see that she can be successful. Address her concerns about not having the "smarts" to succeed and about her lack of self-confidence in being able to stick to it.

_____

_____

_____

_____

_____

_____

GOAL!

Action Items	Check When Done

- Affirmations

- Visualizations—images

- Close your eyes for two minutes and experience the feelings of having achieved your goal

- Day 3's assignment

- Today's scheduled Action Items from your calendar

Countdown: 27 days until you are in the habit of working toward your goal.

DAY 4
No One Goes It Alone

A friend congratulates you on achieving your goal and asks what the keys to success were. You tell your friend one key was the support you received from friends and family. The friend seems interested in hearing more.

Describe the role friends and family played in helping you reach your goal.

_____

_____

_____

_____

_____

_____

_____

Action Items	Check When Done

- Affirmations

- Visualizations—images

- Close your eyes for two minutes and experience the feelings of having achieved your goal

- Day 4's assignment

- Today's scheduled Action Items from your calendar

Countdown: 26 days until you are in the habit of working toward your goal.

DAY 5
Anne Mulcahy, CEO

—Quote for the day—

"Good leadership is about the company's success, not your own."

—Anne Mulcahy

In August 2001, Anne Mulcahy became the first woman CEO in Xerox's history and its first female chairman in January 2002. Her success was not the meteoric rise that many people think a CEO would have, but rather a steady and even-paced progression. Ironically, when the decision was made to name her the new CEO, she was surprised, unlike the vast majority of big-ego CEOs who might have wondered what took so long.

To understand Anne Mulcahy's mind-set, it is important to know her background.

She was born on October 21, 1952, in Rockville Centre, New York, the only daughter in a family with four boys. Anne's parents encouraged her to compete equally with her brothers and this upbringing taught her not only to handle criticism but to listen to it as well—an ability that helped her make difficult decisions. She earned a degree in English and journalism at Marymount College and then spent the next sixteen years working in sales for Xerox. During this time Anne, who had subsequently married and had a family, had frequent thoughts about quitting to spend more time with her two sons.

However, she performed well and the company kept promoting her, first to vice president of human resources in 1992, later to vice president and staff officer of customer operations worldwide, and then in 1998 to senior vice president and chief staff officer. These promotions were then followed by her promotion to president of general market operations.

Anne's steady and thoughtful approach impressed senior management, and in May 2000, the Xerox board picked Mulcahy to be president and CEO-in-waiting. The promotion to CEO came in 2001. "I never expected to be CEO of Xerox. I was never groomed to be CEO of Xerox. It was a total surprise to everyone, including myself," she later said. However, the board saw in her the temperament to lead Xerox out of the doldrums and move forward decisively in order to save the company from its downward sales spiral.

Mulcahy had qualities that Xerox badly needed. She was hardworking, disciplined, and she was fiercely loyal to Xerox—the company, the brand, and the people. It was her straightforwardness that set her apart. Anne's coworkers described her as both compassionate and tough. "Part of her DNA is to tell you the good, the bad, and the ugly," said one colleague. Mulcahy's willingness to work side by side with subordinates gave her unusual credibility and permitted her to lift up the sagging spirits of Xerox employees.

Anne needed all the internal goodwill she could muster, as she began her tenure as CEO by ordering a restructuring of the copying and printing giant, which cut annual expenses by $1.7 billion, slashed 25,000 jobs, and sold $2.3 billion worth of noncore assets to reduce Xerox's long-term debt. Mulcahy also paid a $10 million fine and restated five years of Xerox's revenues to quiet an embarrassing accounting scandal. The Securities and Exchange Commission had accused the company of bending its numbers to meet Wall Street's expectations. Mulcahy was praised by colleagues for achieving a minor miracle through honesty, communication, and a willingness to tackle tough tasks.

Her strong communication skills and her straightforwardness made all the difference in the early days of her reign as president. Mulcahy logged 100,000 miles in visits to far-flung Xerox locations, where she held town-style meetings to address matters such as Xerox's possible bankruptcy and closure. The meetings were quite contentious, but Mulcahy answered all questions as honestly as possible. She managed to boost morale by giving workers a reason to be hopeful and committed to the company. As she later elaborated, "If you schmooze and spin your communications, it comes back to bite you in your ability to establish credibility with people."

Mulcahy saw communication as the most important tool for a leader: "I believe strongly that my success as a leader is driven by my commitment to understanding and meeting customers' requirements as well as developing and nurturing a motivated and proud workforce." Xerox's problems were rooted in the fact that the company had stopped listening to its customers. Fortunately, Mulcahy's background in sales gave her a customer-centric perspective that saved the life of the technology giant. The Company had lost focus on the market. It had neglected to change its cost model, maintaining its strategy despite obvious signs from customers that it no longer worked. Mulcahy, known for being an extremely focused and decisive woman, placed the company's emphasis back on sales and refused to tolerate subordinates who performed poorly.

Xerox bounced back in the initial three years of her tenure as CEO, but by 2004 it had not experienced the kind of growth it had known during its heyday. Mulcahy's solution was to reinvigorate the company by dedicating $1 billion annually to research and development. She planned to expand into consulting services by helping companies better manage their document flow and by setting up computer networks. Analysts expressed doubts that Xerox could change its image and learn new areas, but the firm's stock continued to rise.

Under Mulcahy's leadership, Xerox is one of the best comeback stories of corporate America. Sales have steadily increased to $17.2 billion in 2008, an 8 percent increase over the previous year. The company has a brighter future thanks to the steady leadership of Mulcahy and the focus she placed on color printing and document management.

Anne Mulcahy is a classic example of a leader who valued communications and straightforwardness above all else. These traits paid huge dividends to Anne and contributed to her rating by *FORTUNE* magazine as one of the top executives in the country.

GOAL!

Action Items	Check When Done

- Affirmations

- Visualizations—images

- Close your eyes for two minutes and experience the feelings of having achieved your goal

- Day 5's assignment

- Today's scheduled Action Items from your calendar

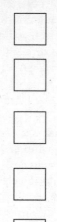

Countdown: 25 days until you are in the habit of working toward your goal.

DAY 6
Your Goal, Now

—Quote for the day—

"It's the greatest shot of adrenaline to be doing what you've wanted to do so badly."

— Charles Lindbergh

You are attending a colleague's retirement party. This is someone you have known and worked with for many years and you value what he has to say. This person is giving a speech which emphasizes the importance of staying focused on what's important, because time passes by so quickly. You feel a sense of peace upon hearing this, knowing you have achieved your goal.

Describe how it feels to know that you have accomplished an important goal.

_____

_____

_____

_____

_____

_____

GOAL!

Action Items	Check When Done

- Affirmations   ☐

- Visualizations—images   ☐

- Close your eyes for two minutes and
  experience the feelings of having
  achieved your goal   ☐

- Day 6's assignment   ☐

- Today's scheduled Action Items from
  your calendar   ☐

Countdown: 24 days until you are in the habit of working toward your goal.

DAY 7
On Your Way Up

—Quote for the day—

"Well begun is half done."

—Aristotle

Think back to the first week of working toward your goal. How did it feel to know you were making progress?

_____

_____

_____

_____

_____

_____

_____

_____

GOAL!

Action Items	Check When Done
• Affirmations	☐
• Visualizations—images	☐
• Close your eyes for two minutes and experience the feelings of having achieved your goal	☐
• Day 7's assignment	☐
• Today's scheduled Action Items from your calendar	☐

Are your affirmations and visualizations still meaningful? If not, change them.

Countdown: 23 days until you are in the habit of working toward your goal.

DAY 8
Action Drives Motivation

"How soon 'not now' becomes 'never.'"

—Martin Luther

You and your coworker started your respective sales goals on the same day. While you have accomplished your goal, your friend has not. Your friend is filled with excuses like "I know I should be making more sales calls, but I'm not in the mood today" or "I've been tired lately and don't have the energy."

List what you have learned about overcoming procrastination to help keep your coworker moving forward.

_____

_____

_____

_____

_____

_____

_____

GOAL!

Action Items	Check When Done

- Affirmations

- Visualizations—images

- Close your eyes for two minutes and experience the feelings of having achieved your goal

- Day 8's assignment

- Today's scheduled Action Items from your calendar

Countdown: 22 days until you are in the habit of working toward your goal.

DAY 9
Attitude of Gratitude

You strike up a conversation with a man at a bus stop. He tells you that it's his first day on the job of his dreams. He says all his hard work has paid off. In a non-arrogant way, he is basking in the glow of reaching his dream. You reflect on the day you accomplished your goal and a sense of accomplishment comes over you. Immediately following that you feel a sense of gratitude. You're surprised by this and give it further thought.

Who are you grateful to and why?

_____

_____

_____

_____

_____

GOAL!

Action Items	Check When Done
• Affirmations	☐
• Visualizations—images	☐
• Close your eyes for two minutes and experience the feelings of having achieved your goal	☐
• Day 9's assignment	☐
• Today's scheduled Action Items from your calendar	☐

Countdown: 21 days until you are in the habit of working toward your goal.

DAY 10
Be True to Yourself

—Quote for the day—

"To Thine Own Self Be True."

—William Shakespeare

A coworker tells you he has decided not to pursue a goal, which just last week he said was a dream of his. The coworker says it is because a family member thought it was not worthwhile. You are surprised at this because you feel quite the opposite.

Give your coworker advice on dealing with negative feedback.

_____

_____

_____

_____

_____

_____

_____

Action Items	**Check When Done**

- Affirmations

- Visualizations—images

- Close your eyes for two minutes and experience the feelings of having achieved your goal

- Day 10's assignment

- Today's scheduled Action Items from your calendar

Countdown: 20 days until you are in the habit of working toward your goal.

DAY 11
Practice Makes Perfect

"Theory looks well on paper, but does not amount to anything without practice."
—Henry Wheeler Shaw

One of the keys to success in reaching your goal was developing the habit of consistently working toward it. Along the way there were times when you were tempted to slack off, even though you knew the importance of being disciplined. One thing that helped you stay on track was the expression "Practice Makes Perfect."

Describe why this saying is relevant to you.

_____

_____

_____

_____

_____

_____

GOAL!

Action Items	Check When Done

- Affirmations ☐

- Visualizations—images ☐

- Close your eyes for two minutes and experience the feelings of having achieved your goal ☐

- Day 11's assignment ☐

- Today's scheduled Action Items from your calendar ☐

Countdown: 19 days until you are in the habit of working toward your goal.

DAY 12
Walt Disney

—Quote for the day—

"All our dreams can come true, if we have the courage to pursue them."

—Walt Disney

Walt Disney, a poor farm boy from Missouri, grew up to realize his dream of entertaining American audiences.

Walt's story begins with his birth in Chicago in 1901, where he was one of five children. Walt quickly became interested in drawing and at the age of seven was selling some of his sketches to the neighbors. In high school he continued his drawing and became interested in photography, both of which he applied to his work on the school paper. Walt furthered his talents by attending the Academy of Fine Arts at night.

Walt's love of drawing/art influenced every aspect of his life. An ambulance driver in World War I, Walt's ambulance was covered with drawings and cartoons instead of camouflage. His passion for his art was evident in everything he did. After the war, Walt got a job in Kansas City as an advertising cartoonist and, in 1920, he began marketing his animated cartoons, later perfecting a new method for combining animation and live action.

In 1923, armed with $40 dollars and a dream, Walt left Kansas City for Hollywood, where his brother Roy would lend encouragement and a modest amount of financial support. In short order, they were able to sell a featurette named the "Alice Comedy" and they used funds from the sale of additional "Alice Comedies" to set up a small production facility in the back of a local real estate office.

Gaining momentum, Walt created Mickey Mouse in 1928 and rode the wave of the new sound technology in film-making. He introduced Mickey in *Steamboat Willie*, the world's first fully synchronized sound cartoon, which premiered in New

York City in November 1928. More great things were to come, as Walt's passion for creating animation and entertaining audiences kept driving him forward.

Walt worked tirelessly to perfect the art of animation. Technicolor was introduced in the early 1930s and, using this technique, Walt won his first of thirty-two personal Academy Awards with the release of *Flowers and Trees* in 1932. *Snow White and the Seven Dwarfs* was introduced in 1937 as the first full-length animated musical feature. The cost for production was close to $1.5 million, a staggering sum since this was during the Great Depression.

Walt's desire to improve the quality of animation always motivated him to do more, and during the next five years he produced such award-winning films as *Pinocchio, Fantasia, Dumbo* and *Bambi*. The success of these movies led to the opening in 1940 of the Disney Studios in Burbank, California.

The same year that World War II came to a close, 1945, brought the release of *The Three Caballeros*, which combined live action with the cartoon medium. This same process was utilized in other films, such as *Song of the South* and *Mary Poppins*. During Walt's lifetime, a total of eighty-one features were produced and released by the studio.

Walt loved children and entertaining, so in 1955 he created Disneyland, where children and adults from around the world were entertained. Walt ventured into television in the mid 1950s and was among the first to create full-color programming. His television shows, *Wonderful World of Color*, *The Mickey Mouse Club*, and *Zorro* were very popular in the late 1950s and early 1960s.

Walt Disney's biggest undertaking was looming on the horizon—his creations of Disney World and EPCOT (Experimental Prototype Community of Tomorrow) opened in Florida in 1971 and 1982, respectively. These theme parks have become two of the world's most popular destinations and are a living testament to Walt Disney's passion for creating wholesome environments that can be enjoyed by people of all ages.

Walt died in 1966 at the age of sixty-five. He followed his passion for art as a young boy and turned it into his life's work. He touched the minds and hearts of countless millions. Walt left behind a legacy in the films he produced and the theme parks he created, all of which will continue to entertain audiences for decades to come. Walt Disney truly followed his dream.

Action Items	**Check When Done**
• Affirmations	☐
• Visualizations—images	☐
• Close your eyes for two minutes and experience the feelings of having achieved your goal	☐
• Day 12's assignment	☐
• Today's scheduled Action Items from your calendar	☐

Countdown: 18 days until you are in the habit of working toward your goal.

DAY 13
No Time Like "Real Time"

"The great French marshall Lyautey once asked his gardener to plant a tree. The gardener objected that the tree was slow growing and would not reach maturity for 100 years. The marshall replied, 'In that case, there is no time to lose; plant it this afternoon!'"

—John F. Kennedy

Someone you know has been talking about a goal that she has wanted to achieve. This discussion has gone on for a while without any action on her part. You know your friend is capable, she just hasn't gotten started.

Convince your friend how important it is to begin working on her goal.

_____

_____

_____

_____

_____

_____

_____

Action Items	Check When Done
• Affirmations	☐
• Visualizations—images	☐
• Close your eyes for two minutes and experience the feelings of having achieved your goal	☐
• Day 13's assignment	☐
• Today's scheduled Action Items from your calendar	☐

Countdown: 17 days until you are in the habit of working toward your goal.

DAY 14
On Target

"Plans are great and so is diverging from them."

—Alice Dustin

Two weeks into the pursuit of your goal you ran into a friend who asked about your progress. He asked "Are you on track?" That question was a revelation because, even though you knew you were making progress, you wondered how closely you were adhering to the plan you created. Before you looked, you made a pact with yourself:

If my plan isn't working I will make the following adjustments.

_____

_____

_____

_____

_____

_____

GOAL!

Action Items	Check When Done
• Affirmations	☐
• Visualizations—images	☐
• Close your eyes for two minutes and experience the feelings of having achieved your goal	☐
• Day 14's assignment	☐
• Today's scheduled Action Items from your calendar	☐

Are your affirmations and visualizations still meaningful? If not, change them.

Countdown: 16 days until you are in the habit of working toward your goal.

DAY 15
Success Is a Good Thing

Your neighbor tells you that he is planning to turn down a promotion at work. While the new job would be a welcome change and provide more money, he would have greater decision-making power and he fears he might not handle it well. In addition, he is concerned about the impact this promotion will have on a close friend, who has been down on his luck lately.

Let him know why he should take the job.

_____

_____

_____

_____

_____

_____

_____

GOAL!

Action Items   **Check When Done**

- Affirmations

- Visualizations—images

- Close your eyes for two minutes and
  experience the feelings of having
  achieved your goal

- Day 15's assignment

- Today's scheduled Action Items from
  your calendar

Countdown: 15 days until you are in the habit of working toward your goal.

DAY 16
You're the Boss

Your former boss, whom you admire, calls you today asking for your advice on overcoming a business problem. He and his staff are tackling a project and feel like they have hit a plateau. Knowing that you recently achieved your goal, they seek your counsel.

Describe what you did when you felt like you reached a plateau and what spurred you to continue on.

_____

_____

_____

_____

_____

_____

Action Items	**Check When Done**

- Affirmations

- Visualizations—images

- Close your eyes for two minutes and experience the feelings of having achieved your goal

- Day 16's assignment

- Today's scheduled Action Items from your calendar

Countdown: 14 days until you are in the habit of working toward your goal.

DAY 17
Changing the Game

—Quote for the day—

"Florida, Florida, Florida."

—Tim Russert

Timothy Russert was a television journalist and lawyer who appeared for more than sixteen years as the moderator of NBC's *Meet the Press*. He was NBC News' Washington bureau chief and also hosted the weekend interview program *Tim Russert*. He was a frequent correspondent and guest on NBC's *The Today Show* and *Hardball*. Russert covered several presidential elections, and he presented the NBC News/*Wall Street Journal* survey on *NBC Nightly News* during the 2008 U.S. presidential election. *TIME* magazine included Russert on its list of the 100 most influential people in the world in 2008.

This larger-than-life figure in political journalism started from very humble beginnings. Timothy John Russert was born in Buffalo, New York, in 1950 to Irish-American Catholic parents: Elizabeth (Betty), a homemaker, and Timothy Joseph "Big Russ" Russert, a sanitation worker and newspaper truck driver. Tim was the second of four children. From his father, he learned the value of hard work. After working one summer on a garbage truck, he also knew that manual labor was not the right line of work for him.

He said that his father, who never finished high school, "worked two jobs all his life so his four kids could go to Catholic school, and those schools changed my life." He also spoke warmly of Catholic nuns who taught him. "Sister Mary Lucille founded a school newspaper and appointed me editor and changed my life," he said. Russert claimed that teachers in Catholic schools "taught me to read and write, but also how to tell right from wrong."

An excellent student, Tim received his B.A. in 1972 from John Carroll University and his law degree, with honors, from the Cleveland-Marshall College of Law in 1976. Russert met Maureen Orth at the 1976 Democratic National Convention; they married in 1983. Their son Luke graduated from Boston College in 2008.

Tim Russert had an early interest in politics. At the age of twenty-eight, he was chosen as special counsel to Senator Daniel Patrick Moynihan of New York and later was selected to run Moynihan's New York City office. All this occurred before he turned thirty. After five years with Moynihan, Tim worked as a counselor to governor Mario M. Cuomo of New York from 1983 to 1984.

Lawrence Grossman, the president of NBC News, was so taken by Russert's grasp of practical politics that he hired him in 1984 as his assistant. Eventually, Russert was appointed chief of the Washington bureau. According to Al Hunt, his colleague and a close friend who first met him during Russert's days working for Moynihan, "He was intrigued by it as a career choice. He absolutely set the standard for moving from politics to journalism. He proved it could be done." All the hard work Russert had performed during his government career was about to pay off.

Behind the scenes, Mr. Russert's colleagues at NBC News soon learned that he had a gift for taking the most complex political situations and making them both understandable and compelling.

"He had a better political insight than anyone else in the room, period," said Jeff Zucker, the chief executive of NBC Universal, who was then an up-and-coming producer.

According to Zucker, Michael Gartner, then president of NBC News, went to Russert at some point in the late 1980s to ask him to be the Washington bureau chief. "Michael came back from the meeting," Zucker recalled, "and said he had also decided to name him the new moderator of *Meet the Press*."

"This was a guy who had no on-camera experience," Zucker said. "Forget that he had never hosted a program. He had never appeared on television."

But Tim was ready when this opportunity presented itself.

Despite the fact that he had no real media training, Russert took over the Sunday morning program *Meet the Press* in 1991, and he would eventually become its longest serving host. The program's name was changed to *Meet the Press with Tim Russert*, and, at his suggestion, went to an hour-long format in 1992. Russert also modified the program to have a greater focus on in-depth interviews with high-profile guests, where he was known especially for his extensive preparatory research.

Tim was always looking for better ways to do things and he constantly tinkered with the show to improve it. One approach he developed was to find old quotes or video clips that were inconsistent with guests' more recent statements, present them on-air to his guests, and then ask them to clarify their positions. This probing was tough on the guests, but it was a hit with viewers. After one particularly contentious Sunday session, Senator John McCain recalled that he told Russert,

"I hadn't had so much fun since my last interrogation in prison camp." The show became increasingly popular, receiving more than four million viewers per week, and it was recognized as one of the most important sources of political news.

Tim made the complex understandable for the vast majority of his viewers. A good example of this was his trademark dry-erase board that he used during NBC's coverage of the 2000 presidential election. Russert calculated possible electoral college outcomes on this white marker board (now in the Smithsonian Institution) on the air and memorably summed up the outcome of the election as dependent upon "Florida, Florida, Florida."

Russert again accurately predicted the final battleground of the presidential elections of 2004: "Ohio, Ohio, Ohio."

Russert was defined as much by what he was not as by what he was. He was not lazy or lax, he was not an ideologue, and he was not a cynic. Beyond his family, Russert's passion was politics, and he cared enough about the game to try to keep it, and its players, honest.

Tim's death in 2008 at age fifty-eight cut short what was an exceptional life of achievement. But he left behind a compelling legacy of how hard work, dedication to his craft, and an insatiable desire to make the complex issues simple for his audience propelled him through a career at which he excelled. Tim is an example of how important it is to be ready for the big break that often comes when least expected, but which can change your life in many dramatic ways.

GOAL!

Action Items   **Check When Done**

- Affirmations

- Visualizations—images

- Close your eyes for two minutes and
  experience the feelings of having
  achieved your goal

- Day 17's assignment

- Today's scheduled Action Items from
  your calendar

Countdown: 13 days until you are in the habit of working toward your goal.

DAY 18
Back on Track

You feel really good about the times when "life" got in the way of your goal, yet you stayed the course. Sometimes it felt like starting over, but you kept moving forward and that makes you feel great.

Describe a setback that you were able to overcome.

_____

_____

_____

_____

_____

_____

_____

GOAL!

Action Items	Check When Done
• Affirmations	☐
• Visualizations—images	☐
• Close your eyes for two minutes and experience the feelings of having achieved your goal	☐
• Day 18's assignment	☐
• Today's scheduled Action Items from your calendar	☐

Are your affirmations and visualizations still meaningful? If not, change them.

Countdown: 12 days until you are in the habit of working toward your goal.

DAY 19

A New Approach

*"The pessimist sees difficulty in every opportunity.
The optimist sees the opportunity in every difficulty."*

—Sir Winston Churchill

A coworker who is normally happy on the job has a new boss. The boss has given him a poor performance evaluation, along with a three-step plan to help him improve. Your coworker is steaming mad and, although he wants to keep his job, is resentful and hurt, and he refuses to act on the plan.

Help him reframe how he is approaching this situation. Arm him with the positive attitude necessary to be successful.

_____

_____

_____

_____

_____

_____

_____

GOAL!

Action Items	Check When Done

- Affirmations ☐

- Visualizations—images ☐

- Close your eyes for two minutes and experience the feelings of having achieved your goal ☐

- Day 19's assignment ☐

- Today's scheduled Action Items from your calendar ☐

Countdown: 11 days until you are in the habit of working toward your goal.

DAY 20

Way to Go

—Quote for the day—

"Arriving at one point is the starting point to another."

—John Dewey

A colleague who has been working diligently on an important goal has reached a milestone. Upon learning this, you decide to acknowledge her achievement. You send her an e-mail with the subject line, "Way to go!"

Write the e-mail:

_____

_____

_____

_____

_____

_____

_____

_____

GOAL!

Action Items	Check When Done
• Affirmations	☐
• Visualizations—images	☐
• Close your eyes for two minutes and experience the feelings of having achieved your goal	☐
• Day 20's assignment	☐
• Today's scheduled Action Items from your calendar	☐

Countdown: 10 days until you are in the habit of working toward your goal.

DAY 21
Me in Three Years

"When it comes to the future, there are three kinds of people: those who let it happen, those who make it happen, and those who wonder what happened."
—John M. Richardson, Jr.

Write a letter to yourself, to be opened in three years, listing the things you plan on accomplishing in that period of time.

_____

Date _____

A Letter to Myself,

When I open this letter three years from today, I will have accomplished the following:

_____

_____

_____

_____

Sincerely,
Me

_____

Cut this letter out, seal it, and do not open it until three years from today.

GOAL!

Action Items	**Check When Done**
• Affirmations	☐
• Visualizations—images	☐
• Close your eyes for two minutes and experience the feelings of having achieved your goal	☐
• Day 21's assignment	☐
• Today's scheduled Action Items from your calendar	☐

Are your affirmations and visualizations still meaningful? If not, change them.

Countdown: 9 days until you are in the habit of working toward your goal.

DAY 22

Off-Line

"You measure the size of the accomplishment by the obstacles you had to overcome to reach your goals."

—Booker T. Washington

You run into your former boss, who you haven't seen in many years, and the two of you go off for coffee. This person has always believed in your abilities. He asks how you are doing and you are eager to tell him that you have just achieved an important goal. It's just the kind of thing this person would love to hear about.

Tell him about your goal, how important it was to you, the difficulties you have had to overcome, and how it feels now that you've accomplished it.

_____

_____

_____

_____

_____

_____

_____

_____

GOAL!

Action Items	Check When Done

- Affirmations

- Visualizations—images

- Close your eyes for two minutes and
  experience the feelings of having
  achieved your goal

- Day 22's assignment

- Today's scheduled Action Items from
  your calendar

Countdown: 8 days until you are in the habit of working toward your goal.

DAY 23
Pushing Forward

"Difficulties mastered are opportunities won."

—Sir Winston Churchill

Think of a time in the past when you pushed forward and reached a goal. Describe what contributed to your success.

_____

_____

_____

_____

_____

_____

_____

_____

_____

GOAL !

Action Items	Check When Done

- Affirmations ☐

- Visualizations—images ☐

- Close your eyes for two minutes and experience the feelings of having achieved your goal ☐

- Day 23's assignment ☐

- Today's scheduled Action Items from your calendar ☐

Countdown: 7 days until you are in the habit of working toward your goal.

DAY 24
Tape Breakers

"Work is either fun or drudgery. It depends on your attitude. I like fun."
—Colleen C. Barrett

Some people fall over the finish line and others break through the tape. They still reached the same point, but one has more enthusiasm than the other. Because of that energy, the tape breaker is inspired to take on a new challenge. Which one were you when you crossed the finish line and why?

_____

_____

_____

_____

_____

_____

_____

_____

GOAL!

Action Items	Check When Done

- Affirmations ☐

- Visualizations—images ☐

- Close your eyes for two minutes and experience the feelings of having achieved your goal ☐

- Day 24's assignment ☐

- Today's scheduled Action Items from your calendar ☐

Countdown: 6 days until you are in the habit of working toward your goal.

DAY 25

Swing for the Fences

You are a commencement speaker at a college graduation. The focus of your speech is to encourage the students to aim high. Talk to them about the importance of setting aggressive goals and how each student has the potential to achieve great things.

Dear Graduates:

_____

_____

_____

_____

_____

_____

_____

_____

_____

GOAL!

Action Items	**Check When Done**

- Affirmations

- Visualizations—images

- Close your eyes for two minutes and experience the feelings of having achieved your goal

- Day 25's assignment

- Today's scheduled Action Items from your calendar

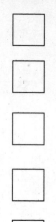

Countdown: 5 days until you are in the habit of working toward your goal.

DAY 26
Giving Back

—Quote for the day—

"I must admit that I personally measure success in terms of the contributions an individual makes to her or his fellow human beings."

—Margaret Mead

You have wanted to volunteer your time to an organization similar to Junior Achievement. This will give you an opportunity to inspire students about the workplace and how they can be successful in the business world.

Complete the following application:

List five things you value.

_____

_____

_____

_____

_____

List five things you do well.

_____

_____

_____

_____

_____

Take the ten things you have listed above and turn them into an explanation of why you would make an excellent mentor for Junior Achievement.

_____

_____

_____

_____

_____

_____

_____

_____

_____

Action Items	Check When Done
• Affirmations	☐
• Visualizations—images	☐
• Close your eyes for two minutes and experience the feelings of having achieved your goal	☐
• Day 26's assignment	☐
• Today's scheduled Action Items from your calendar	☐

Countdown: 4 days until you are in the habit of working toward your goal.

DAY 27
It Can Be Done

—Quote for the day—

"I am looking for a lot of men who have an infinite capacity to not know what can't be done."

—Henry Ford

You overhear a conversation in which one person says to the other, "They'll never find a cure for Alzheimer's." You instinctively know that's not true. How does it feel to know that you believe in the power of possibilities?

_____

_____

_____

_____

_____

_____

_____

_____

GOAL!

Action Items   **Check When Done**

- Affirmations

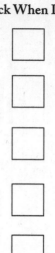

- Visualizations—images

- Close your eyes for two minutes and
  experience the feelings of having
  achieved your goal

- Day 27's assignment

- Today's scheduled Action Items from
  your calendar

Have you contacted your support or accountability partner lately?

Countdown: 3 days until you are in the habit of working toward your goal.

DAY 28
New Perspective

"The greater danger for most of us is not that our aim is too high and we miss, but that it is too low and we reach it."

—Michelangelo

You are now thinking of yourself and your world differently, recognizing how much more is possible than you thought before. You feel empowered now and can use this motivation in many positive ways.

What further goals spring to mind?

_____

_____

_____

_____

_____

_____

GOAL!

Action Items	Check When Done
• Affirmations	☐
• Visualizations—images	☐
• Close your eyes for two minutes and experience the feelings of having achieved your goal	☐
• Day 28's assignment	☐
• Today's scheduled Action Items from your calendar	☐

Are your affirmations and visualizations still meaningful? If not, change them.

Countdown: 2 days until you are in the habit of working toward your goal.

DAY 29
Distinguished from Your Peers

"To follow without halt, one aim; there is the secret of success. And success? What is it? I do not find it in the applause of the theater; it lies rather in the satisfaction of accomplishment."

—Anna Pavlova

You win an award for outstanding achievement in your field. The race was close and the competition was impressive. A local reporter covering the story asks you to describe your keys to success.

Write down your response.

_____

_____

_____

_____

_____

_____

_____

GOAL!

Action Items   **Check When Done**

- Affirmations

- Visualizations—images

- Close your eyes for two minutes and
  experience the feelings of having
  achieved your goal

- Day 29's assignment

- Today's scheduled Action Items from
  your calendar

Countdown: 1 day until you are in the habit of working toward your goal.

DAY 30
Success

"Great things are done by a series of small things brought together."
—Vincent van Gogh

Make a toast to yourself, as today is a significant day. Give yourself credit for following through and creating the habit of working toward your goal. It is a milestone that should be acknowledged and celebrated. Congratulations! You have laid the groundwork for this goal and future goals.

As you have done for the past month, continue persistently until you reach your goal:

GOAL!

Action Items	Check When Done

Action Items

Check When Done

- Affirmations

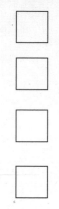

- Visualizations—images

- Close your eyes for two minutes and experience the feelings of having achieved your goal

- Today's scheduled Action Items from your calendar

Afterword

Congratulations, you have completed the 30-DAY GOAL TRACK. By now, you have either achieved your goal, or you are well on your way to doing so.

If Your Goal Is Completed

Your goal may have been one of those that can be achieved in thirty days. If this is the case, take a moment to fully acknowledge the magnitude of your accomplishment. Too many of us have the tendency to minimize the importance of what we accomplish, especially if our goal only took a month to achieve. Now that you have successfully reached your goal, it can serve as a springboard to tackling new goals that are important to you. If you are ready to start on a new goal:

- Use a separate piece of paper and answer all the questions presented in the book as they relate to your new goal.
- Use the Goal Planning Worksheet as a template to list your new Action Items and then schedule them in your calendar.
- Create a new vision board.

Buy a journal to record your answers to the exercises in the 30-DAY GOAL TRACK. While you already know what the exercises are, your responses may vary from the previous entries. Some people would rather have a fresh copy of the book, so consider purchasing another one. Do whatever is most effective for you.

If Your Goal Continues

Many goals are long-term ones. To keep yourself motivated, you may want to create a new vision board to keep things fresh. The exercises in the 30-DAY GOAL TRACK can continue to serve you. Simply review your previous responses one day at a time. If you would like to redo the exercises, you can buy a journal to write your responses, or buy a fresh copy of *GOAL!*

Final Thoughts

Whether you have completed your goal or are continuing onward, the important thing is that you are living life to the fullest. Truly, nothing can stand in your way.

Now that you have successfully made the journey to one special place, there are other ports of call yet to be explored. All great successes begin with a dream, followed by your efforts to achieve it. Go for it!

Gladys Stone is an executive coach and recruiter who injects a dose of adrenaline into corporations and individuals to empower them to perform at higher levels. She zeroes in on the areas of negotiations, higher productivity, and effective leadership. Her company, Whelan Stone (www.whelanstone.com) was founded in 1999 and works primarily with Fortune 500 companies, recruiting high-impact talent and boosting the performance level of management. Whelan Stone is driven to help clients increase their competitive edge in order to achieve their goals, and has been frequently quoted in the *Wall Street Journal*, *Fortune* magazine, *USA Today*, and the *Boston Globe*. Gladys authors a cutting-edge career blog on The Huffington Post website, which is packed with new ideas on how to tackle workplace issues.

Gladys has a B.A. from San Francisco State University. In her off hours she is a playwright.

Fred Whelan is founder of Whelan Stone (www.whelanstone.com), an executive recruiting and coaching firm, headquartered in San Francisco. His company acts as a catalyst to Fortune 500 clients to accelerate the development of their management teams in the areas of: project management, high performance team development, and effective communications. Years of coaching has enabled Fred to harness the latent talents of individuals and bring them to the forefront in a dynamic and productive way. His advice is frequently sought after by the media, such as *USA Today*, the *Wall Street Journal*, *Fortune* magazine, and the *Boston Globe*. He also writes a career blog on The Huffington Post website, which inspires people to new levels of achievement.

Fred earned a B.A. from The University of Delaware and an MBA from the Wharton Graduate School of the University of Pennsylvania. In his spare time he enjoys reading biographies and historic accounts, especially those about the Civil War.